RECIPES
FROM MY
KITCHEN

101 Indian and Continental Recipes

D1784260

MARY ANN GEORGE

INDIA • SINGAPORE • MALAYSIA

Notion Press Media Pvt Ltd

No. 50, Chettiyar Agaram Main Road,
Vanagaram, Chennai, Tamil Nadu – 600 095

First Published by Notion Press 2021
Copyright © Mary Ann George 2021
All Rights Reserved.

ISBN
Paperback 978-1-68538-944-4
Hardcase 978-1-63904-680-5

Thank you Lord Almighty for your many blessings.
Dedicated to my family and friends.

"If you are what you eat, then I only
want to eat the good stuff."
~ Remy the rat from Ratatouille

Contents

SALADS, APPETIZERS & STARTERS

MAINS

SIDES & CURRIES

SWEETS & DESSERTS

ACCOMPANIMENTS

Acknowledgments

 From a young age, I have been an avid collector of recipes of all types. My mother, Nirmala already had a fascinating compilation of recipes, to which my sister Tania and I added to over the years. Some of them were cut-outs from magazines or notes from cooking classes but most were shared by family and friends. Over time, with changes in houses and one of us always moving cities, the recipe collections also moved along with us.

This however led to a permanent treasure hunt for the priceless recipe books. There would be calls back and forth going *"Is the orange recipe diary with you?"* or *"Is the blue file of recipe cut outs in Kochi, Dubai or Bangalore?"* There were also the desperate calls to mom to find out how exactly to prepare a particular dish; just like the way it was prepared at home. Taking recipe notes over the phone did not always end well and of course, if it didn't turn out right it was mom's fault!

Seeing this perpetual comedy play out, it was my husband Rajiv's idea to put it all together in the form of a book. Thanks to the lockdown and his constant push, this book is a finally a reality.

With this book I would like to thank all of my family, especially those who have shared their recipes with me, cooked meals for me and for all the love and dinner table conversations that we have had over the years. It has been my honor and privilege to sit at your tables and eat those *"appams with crisp edge"* from your wonderful kitchens.

To my ever supportive husband Rajiv, thank you for always loving everything I make, even the burnt meals! This book would not have seen the light of day without my mother Nirmala and sister, Tania. Thank you for sharing and testing out these recipes and mostly for being just a call away. A special mention for my dad for the no holds barred critical analysis of my dishes. You help me aim for the best. I would also like to thank my in-laws for all their encouragement and good wishes.

Special thanks to the Notionpress team who made this dream book come true. Many thanks to the Shutterstock, Icon Finder and The Noun Project websites, which provided the visuals used in this book.

Last but not the least, this book is a testament to all the wonderful cooks in my immediate and extended family. Every get-together was made special by the fabulous treats prepared by the grandmoms, aunts, cousins and kitchen helps who have added their own remarkable dishes to the repertoire. With food being a central part of our family get-togethers; it is not surprising that the next generation also has taken a keen interest in cooking and baking. I would like to thank everyone who has been a part of this culinary journey of mine.

– **Mary Ann George**

Foreword

They say that the way to a man's heart is through his stomach and that holds true for me as well. My better half Mary Ann is a wonderful cook and her passion for trying out new recipes is something that I have always admired. She spends a lot of time and effort in order to cook up a new dish and loves experimenting with recipes. She obsessively watches cooking based television shows where she learns about new cuisines and new methods of cooking.

I am extremely proud of Mary Ann for having compiled this wonderful book during the ongoing lockdown period. She is openly sharing her culinary learnings and experiences with others through this book. I also really like the way that she has structured this book into five different sections namely.

1. Salads, Appetizers & Starters

2. Mains

3. Sides & Curries

4. Sweets & Desserts

5. Accompaniments

I'm a complete foodie and absolutely love having a good meal. The ironic part is that I don't even know the basics of cooking! I do hope to pick up some of these important skills from Mary Ann eventually. I must confess that I learnt a lot about the nuances of cooking after helping Mary Ann put this book together.

As they say, a family that eats together stays together. Food is such a strong way for a family to bond. For Mary Ann and me, our regular date nights are something that we truly cherish. We used to visit restaurants and cafes every once in a while to try out different cuisines. These moments were some of the best memories that we have had together.

I hope that this cook book inspires you the discerning reader to try out a few recipes from this treasured collection that Mary Ann has put together so thoughtfully and painstakingly.

– Rajiv Mathew

Introduction

 This book is an assortment of everyday recipes that have been tried and tested in my family kitchen over the years. Many of these recipes are from the Kerala cuisine, as this is what we generally prepare at home. This is the taste that I have grown to know and love since my childhood days. These recipes are not only from my own kitchen, but also from the kitchens of my family and extended family members which they have generously shared.

For this simple reason, I thought it was important to keep a record of the recipes not only for my sake, but also for the coming generations in my family. Malayali cooking is made up of simple set spices, a little bit of coconut and lots of curry leaves. It is important to get the right combination of spices, timing of when to add what and how long to cook at each step. I also love experimenting with continental cuisines and recreating dishes that I've had at various restaurants/cafes.

This book has a mix of quick & easy recipes and a few elaborate ones. I'm sure that these dishes and the way they are prepared will remind you of your own family recipes. I earnestly hope that you will enjoy some of these dishes as much as my family and I do. Bon appétit!

Salads, Appetizers & Starters

Healthy Quinoa Salad

If you are like me and love salads, then you should definitely try this out. Even if you don't fancy salads, this might just change your mind. This is a refreshing and healthy salad that goes well if you are on a diet. If you are not a fan of some of the ingredients, you can simply opt them out. This recipe is inspired by the Quinoa salad at 'French Toast', a quaint little bistro in Cochin.

Ingredients

- Quinoa (¼ cup)
- Water (½ cup)
- Onion (2 tbsp, diced)
- Cherry tomatoes/sundried tomatoes (2 tbsp)
- Cucumber (2 tbsp, cubed)
- Olives (1 tbsp, sliced)
- Greens – Spring onion/coriander leaves (¼ cup, chopped)
- Green chilli (1, finely chopped)
- Cooked chickpeas (½ cup)
- Fruits – diced mango/pomegranate (3 tbsp)
- Any type of nuts – walnuts/peanuts
- Any type of seeds – melon/pumpkin/sunflower seeds (a handful)
- Any cheese – Feta/cottage cheese/cheddar (crumbled)

Ingredients for the Dressing

- Olive oil (2 tsp)
- Balsamic vinegar (¾ tsp)
- Fresh lemon juice (1 tsp)
- Yellow mustard paste (¼ tsp)
- Salt (¼ tsp)
- Black pepper (½ tsp)

Method

1. Cook quinoa with a pinch of salt in double the quantity of water. Bring it to a boil, cover and simmer on low heat for 12-15 minutes until all the water is gone. Uncover, fluff and cool.

2. Make the dressing, by mixing all in a bowl.

3. Prep all the veggies.

4. Mix the quinoa, veggies, chickpeas and dressing and give a good toss.

5. Taste, adjust salt and lemon to your liking. Serve immediately.

Bruchetta

Pronounced broo•skeh•tuh, it is an Italian appetizer, that is fun and easy to prepare. It consists of grilled bread topped with marinated tomatoes. You can make it interesting by trying out a variety of toppings. Make sure that you use good quality ingredients to prepare this dish, because that makes all the difference.

Ingredients

- Baguette loaf (1)
- Butter (softened, as needed)
- Garlic (5 cloves, finely minced)
- Tomatoes (6, diced)
- Extra virgin olive oil (2 tbsp + extra for drizzling)
- Balsamic vinegar (1 tbsp)
- Black pepper powder
- Mint leaves/oregano/mixed herbs (2 tbsp, finely chopped)
- Salt

Method

1. Cut the baguette diagonally into half inch thick slices. Mix half of the minced garlic with sufficient butter and spread on the slices.

2. Toast in the oven or *tava* for 5 minutes, until it turns golden brown.

3. In the meanwhile, dice the tomatoes, drain off the excess liquid and transfer it to a bowl.

4. Season the tomatoes with balsamic vinegar, extra virgin olive oil, the remaining minced garlic, salt, ground pepper, mint or oregano. Set aside to marinate for 20 minutes.

5. Place the tomato mixture (without the extra liquid) on the toasted baguette slices. Season with additional salt and pepper if required, a generous drizzle of olive oil and serve immediately.

Note

- Topping options: Sundried tomatoes, feta cheese, olives, mushrooms, bacon, capsicum, guacamole, basil, thyme, rosemary. Choose as many or as few as you'd like.

Chicken Croquette

On Sundays, an old lady would set up a freshly fried cutlet stall outside our church. It was so popular that people would form a queue outside her stall even before the mass got over. Even I would make a mental note of whether her stall was up before entering the church! With the attention straying the wrong way, the church decided to do away with the cutlet stall. That's when I decided to try making these awesome cutlets at home; and they taste just as good!

Ingredients

- Boneless chicken (500 grams, minced)
- Onion (3 large, finely chopped or minced)
- Green chilli (3, finely chopped)
- Ginger paste (1½ tsp)
- Garlic paste (1½ tsp)
- Garam masala (1 tsp)
- Pepper powder (1 tsp)
- Turmeric powder (½ tsp)
- Potato (2, large)
- Bread crumbs (2 cups)
- Egg (1, beaten)
- Oil (for sautéing and frying)
- Salt to taste

Method

1. In a non-stick or heavy bottomed pan, sauté the finely chopped onions, green chilli, ginger and garlic in 3-4 tablespoon oil till the onions turn light brown.

2. Now add the minced chicken and sprinkle garam masala powder, pepper powder, turmeric powder and salt.

3. Stir the mixture well till it becomes very dry, or else the cutlet will break apart while frying. Remove to a bowl and set aside.

4. Boil potato with a bit of salt and mash it well. Ensure that there are no lumps.

5. Mix the chicken mixture and boiled potato and form small oval croquettes or patties.

6. Dip each piece into lightly beaten egg and coat with breadcrumbs to cover all sides.

7. Repeat till all the filling is used up. At this point, you can either freeze the patties for future use or fry them right away.

8. Heat oil in a frying pan. When the oil is hot, drop in 2-3 pieces, reduce heat to medium flame and fry till golden brown on all sides.

9. Remove onto a paper towel lined plate to drain excess oil. Serve hot.

Note

- You can use cooked and finely shredded chicken meat instead of raw minced chicken.

Creamy Chicken Sandwich

 I love a good chicken sandwich! It makes for a great lunch box snack or a picnic basket treat on a long road trip. I even prepared this for our church fete and it was sold out in minutes. This is my attempt to recreate the chicken sandwich from 'The Oven', a long standing popular bake house in Cochin.

Ingredients for the Sandwich

- Oil (1 tbsp)
- Garlic paste (1 tsp)
- Boneless chicken (250 grams, marinated with salt, pepper and ginger-garlic paste)
- Black pepper powder (¼ tsp)
- Butter (optional)
- Bread slices (6)
- Salt

Ingredients for the Dressing

- Mayonnaise (¾ cup)
- Fresh Cream (¼ cup)
- Tomato ketchup (3 tbsp)
- Mustard sauce (1 tsp, optional)
- Black pepper powder (½ tsp)
- Chopped herbs – oregano/dill/basil/chives
- Iceberg lettuce (2 cups, chopped)

Method

1. Heat oil in a non-stick pan. Add garlic paste, boneless chicken, black pepper powder and salt. Mix the spices and chicken. Cover and cook for 10 minutes on low heat.

2. When it cools down, shred the chicken using a fork or your hands.

3. Mix the tomato ketchup, cream, mayonnaise, mustard sauce, black pepper powder and herbs. Add the chicken and chopped lettuce.

4. Take bread slices and cut off the edges. Place the chicken-mayo mix in between the two slices of buttered (optional) bread.

Note

- Instead of shredding the chicken manually, you can add the cooked chicken, cream, mayonnaise, sauces and seasoning to the blender and pulse for a few seconds.

- Optional toppings – caramelized onions, fried tomato and cheese.

Strawberry, Spinach & Cheese Salad

 This is a colorful summer salad that you will love! The recipe was shared by my sister Tania who often experiments with a variety of dishes and then shares her best finds. This a versatile salad that you can adapt based on what is available in your kitchen.

Ingredients

- Olive oil (¼ cup)
- Balsamic vinegar (¼ cup)
- Honey (1 tbsp)
- Greens – Baby spinach/romaine lettuce (3-4 cups, chopped)
- Strawberry (1 cup, chopped)
- Green apple (1, cut into 1 inch cubes)
- Any cheese – Feta/cottage cheese/cheddar (150 grams, crumbled)
- Almonds or walnuts (½ cup)
- Sugar (3-4 tbsp)
- Salt

Method

1. To make the dressing, pour olive oil, honey and balsamic vinegar into a jar and shake well. Add seasoning.

2. To make candied almonds; heat the sugar in a pan. As the sugar begins to caramelize, add almonds and a pinch of salt.

3. Let the caramelized sugar coat the almonds. Remove from heat, pour this on to a buttered surface and allow it to cool completely. Gently crush or break into pieces.

4. Toss the spinach, strawberry, apple and cheese with the salad dressing.

5. Sprinkle a generous dose of caramelized nuts. Serve immediately.

Parippu Vada

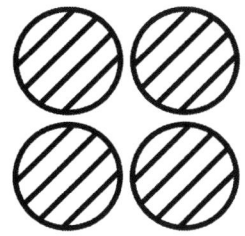

Quintessentially, a Kerala tea stall staple, this snack is best enjoyed on a road trip stop over at a *thattukada* (road side food cart). During my childhood days, I distinctly remember that these were sold on several railways station platforms. Recently my aunt Vimala sent us some yummy homemade *parippu vadas*. It doesn't matter whether you are in the comfort of your home, at a *thattukada* or railway station, served along with *chaaya* (tea), this is an unbeatable combo for your 4:00 pm break!

Ingredients

- *Toor dal* (1 cup)
- Ginger (1 inch, finely chopped)
- Green chilli (2, finely chopped)
- Chilli powder (½ tsp)
- Shallots (10 to 12)
- Curry leaves (1 sprig)
- Oil
- Salt

Method

1. Soak *dal* in water for two hours and drain it well.

2. Keep 1 tablespoon of dal aside and grind it to a coarse paste. Do not add any extra water.

3. Add the remaining dal, chopped ginger, green chillies, chilli powder, curry leaves, shallots and salt to this and mix well.

4. Now form equal sized semi flat *vadas*.

5. Pour sufficient oil to deep fry. Once the oil is heated up, reduce the flame and fry the *vadas* till both sides are golden brown in color.

6. Serve with piping hot tea.

Fried Egg Canapé

 These bread canapés can be made in a jiffy and require only staple ingredients that you will always have in your kitchen. The bread is topped with an egg mix, fried to a golden brown and topped with a dollop of ketchup. Well, what's not to love about fried bread, right? This is a quick snack that my mom makes whenever there is an unannounced visitor at our place.

Ingredients

- Bread slices (4)
- Onion (1, finely chopped)
- Eggs (2)
- Green chilli (2, finely chopped)
- Corn flour (1 tsp)
- Pepper (½ tsp)
- Tomato ketchup (4 tbsp)
- Oil (for shallow fry)
- Salt (¼ tsp)

Method

1. Cut each bread slice into 4 squares.

2. In a mixing bowl, beat together eggs, corn flour, onions, green chilli, salt and pepper.

3. In a frying pan, take enough oil to shallow fry.

4. Pour a spoon of the egg mix onto the bread and immediately put it into the oil, egg side facing into the oil.

5. Flip when the egg gets cooked. Wait for the bread to turn golden brown. This needs to be done quickly, as the bread can easily burn over high heat.

6. Remove from oil and place on a paper towel to drain off the excess oil.

7. Put a dollop of tomato ketchup on the centre of each piece and serve hot.

Vegetable Cutlet

 During the season of Lent, we usually take a break from consuming non-vegetarian dishes. This is when we turn to the evergreen vegetable cutlets. We make these ahead in large quantity and freeze them, so that we can take it out whenever needed for frying. With the addition of soya in these cutlets, you will hardly miss your meat cutlets! These are a must try for those of you who love vegetarian options!

Ingredients

- Carrot (2)
- Beetroot (1, medium sized)
- Cabbage (quarter of 1)
- Soya chunks (1 cup)
- Potato (2)
- Onion (2 large, finely chopped)
- Ginger garlic paste (1 tsp)
- Green chilli (3, chopped)
- Green peas (½ cup)
- Paneer (1 cup, grated, optional)
- Turmeric powder (½ tsp)
- Pepper powder (1 tsp)
- Cumin powder (½ tsp)

- Garam masala (1 tsp)
- Bread crumbs (1 cup)
- Eggs (1, beaten)
- Oil for frying
- Salt to taste

Method

1. Soak the soya chunks in hot water for 30 minutes. Drain the water and squeeze off excess water from the chunks properly. Grind this to a coarse paste. Again squeeze out all the water.

2. Boil the potato with salt and mash until there are no lumps.

3. In a food processor, finely mince the vegetables – carrot, cabbage and beetroot.

4. Heat oil in a pan; add chopped onions, ginger garlic paste, green chillies and sauté till the onions turn translucent.

5. Add pepper powder, garam masala, cumin seed powder and sauté for 1 minute.

6. Add the minced vegetables, green peas and salt. Cover and cook on low heat until they are done and all the water has completely evaporated.

7. Once the vegetable mixture has cooled, add the mashed potato, grated paneer and soya. Mix well using your hands. The mixture should hold shape when rolled into balls.

8. Form small patties. Dip each of the cutlets in beaten egg and roll them in breadcrumbs, making sure that all sides are evenly coated.

9. Deep fry the cutlets over medium flame till they become golden brown.

Note

- If you don't have a food processor or mincer; you can pressure cook all the vegetables and then mash them, but some of the nutrient content will be lost when you drain the remaining water.

Bread Cups

The best thing about this dish is that you can load it with anything you like. The bread is molded into the shape of a cup, into which you can add various fillings. Some of the other filling options that you can try are wilted spinach, capsicum, bacon and cheese. These are available at several of the local bakeries but I would any day recommend homemade bread cups!

Ingredients

- Bread slices (6)
- Butter (4 tbsp)
- Egg (2)
- Cream (2/3 cup)
- Black pepper powder (½ tsp)
- Oregano (½ tsp)
- Chicken sausages (cooked and chopped into ½ inch pieces)
- Onion (½ cup, cubed)
- Capsicum (¼, cubed)
- Grated cheese (optional)
- Salt to taste

Method

1. Flatten the bread slices with a rolling pin.

2. Lightly butter the slices and place it inside greased tart pans or cupcake pan and toast in the oven for 3 minutes. This is done so that the bread does not soak up egg and cream.

3. In a separate bowl, whisk the eggs, cream, salt, pepper and oregano. Add chopped sausage, capsicum and onion.

4. Take the toasted bread out of the oven and spoon the mix into the cups. Additionally, you can top it with cheese.

5. Bake the bread cups in a preheated oven at 180 degrees centigrade for 12 minutes, until the top is lightly golden and the filling is set.

6. Remove from oven and rest for 5 minutes before serving. Serve warm!

Grilled Prawns

 This lip smacking dish is usually made with large tiger prawns. If you get only small prawns, you can skewer 2 or 3 prawns onto each stick. The marination process is critical as it adds the needed spices to the prawns. This dish works as a great appetizer for parties! After all, who can resist grilled prawns on one hand and a drink on the other?

Ingredients for Marination

- Large prawns (12)
- Black pepper powder (1 tsp)
- Turmeric powder (½ tsp)
- Garlic paste (2 tsp)
- Chilli powder (1½ tsp)
- Coconut oil (1 tsp)
- Lime juice (1 tsp)
- Salt to taste

Other Ingredients

- Oil for grilling (3 tbsp)
- Mini skewers (12)
- Lemon wedges (2)

Method

1. Wash, peel and devein (remove the main central vein) the prawn, but keep the tail on.

2. Marinate the prawn for 20 minutes.

3. Now skewer the prawns onto each stick.

4. Heat oil in a *tava* or grill pan. Now place the skewer into the pan and fry the prawns for 3-4 minutes, turning halfway through until just cooked. You may need to do this in batches.

5. Squeeze the lemon wedges over the prawns, before serving.

Roasted Potato Salad

 If you like eggs, potato and bacon (who doesn't?) you will love this version of potato salad. What makes it special is that the potatoes are roasted to a crisp, before adding to the salad. Every bite of this salad is simply scrumptious! This is highly recommended when you are hungry and need some good comfort food!

Ingredients for the Potatoes

- Baby potatoes (300 grams, with skin, cut into half)
- Pepper (½ tsp)
- Olive oil (1-2 tbsp)
- Salt (1 tsp)

Ingredients for the Salad

- Onion (1, diced)
- Bacon (6 strips, fried and diced)
- Eggs (2, hard boiled)
- Mayonnaise (½ cup)
- Yellow mustard paste (½ tsp)
- Dill herb (1 tsp)
- Pepper (½ tsp)
- Coriander leaves or oregano (optional)
- Salt (½ tsp)

Method

1. Sprinkle the halved potatoes with salt, pepper and olive oil. Toss the potatoes and make sure every piece is coated.

2. Place the potatoes in an aluminum foil lined pan and bake in a pre heated oven at 220 degrees centigrade for 30-40 minutes or until the potatoes are crispy. Turn once half-way through baking. Allow it to cool completely.

3. To prepare the salad; in a large bowl add potatoes, onion, bacon, eggs, mayonnaise, mustard paste, dill, oregano, salt and pepper. Gently stir all the ingredients until fully combined.

4. This can be served warm or chilled. If refrigerating, place in an airtight container.

Fish Fingers with Tartar Sauce

Golden and crispy, these crumb coated fish pieces with the slightly tangy tartar sauce is a marvelous combination. You can use any type of filleted fish to prepare this dish. Tartar sauce is a condiment made of mayo and chopped pickles. You can also enhance the sauce by adding herbs or olives.

Ingredients for Marination

- Fish fillets (300 grams)
- Lime juice (1 tbsp)
- Red chilli flakes (½ tsp)
- Black pepper powder (½ tsp)
- Ginger garlic paste (1 tsp)
- Salt (½ tsp)

Ingredients for Coating

- Plain flour (2 tbsp)
- Corn flour (2 tsp)
- Eggs (1, lightly beaten)
- Bread crumbs (1 cup)
- Oil

Ingredients for the Tartar Sauce

- Mayonnaise (½ cup)
- Pickled cucumber (1 tbsp, finely chopped)
- Olives (1 tbsp, finely chopped)
- Lime juice (1 tbsp)
- Fresh dill (1 tbsp, chopped)
- Mustard sauce (½ tsp)
- Black pepper powder
- Salt to taste

Method

1. For the tartar sauce; get a mixing bowl and combine all the above mentioned ingredients and refrigerate.
2. For the fish fingers; cut the fillets into strips.
3. Mix all the ingredients for marination. Coat the fish fillets and keep aside for 20 minutes.
4. In another bowl; mix plain flour and corn flour. Coat the fish in the flour mix.
5. Dip it in beaten egg and coat the fingers with lightly toasted bread crumbs.
6. Heat 4-5 cups of oil for frying in a medium size pan. Once the oil is hot, simmer the heat to medium. Deep fry the fish fingers until golden brown.
7. Serve hot with the tartar sauce.

Note

- To make pickled cucumber; soak thinly sliced English cucumber in brine made of apple cider vinegar (½ cup), water (½ cup), sugar (1 tbsp) and salt (1½ tsp) for 1 hour.

Meat Buns

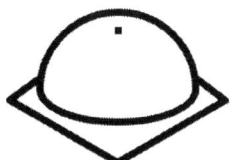 The kitchen smells heavenly when these meat buns come out of the oven. They are soft and perfectly golden brown on top. My husband Rajiv adores these and can gobble up 3 or 4 of these within a few minutes. This is a must try snack for all the hardcore foodies out there.

Ingredients for the Bun

- Dry yeast (2 tsp)
- Warm water (2 tbsp)
- Milk (½ cup)
- Oil (½ cup)
- Sugar (¼ cup)
- Plain flour (2 cups + extra if required)
- Egg (1, beaten)
- Egg white (1, for egg wash)
- White sesame seeds (for sprinkling)
- Salt to taste

Ingredients for the Filling

- Ground beef (400 grams, uncooked)
- Oil (2 tbsp)
- Onion (2, chopped)
- Ginger garlic paste (2 tsp)
- Green chilli (2, diced)
- Pepper powder (1 tsp)
- Fennel powder (½ tsp)
- Chilli powder (½ tsp)
- Turmeric powder (½ tsp)
- Tomato (1, diced)

Method to make the Filling

1. Sauté the onion, ginger garlic paste and green chilli in oil. When the onions turn translucent, add all the *masala* powders.

2. When the powders have roasted, add the diced tomato and let it cook.

3. Add the minced beef and mix well. Cover and cook till the meat is browned and the mix is dry.

4. Take it off the fire and let it cool. Use it for filling the dough.

Method to make the Bun

1. Dissolve the yeast in warm water with half tablespoon sugar and set aside for 10 minutes.

2. Boil the milk and allow it to cool down till it is warm to touch.

3. Then, add the remaining sugar, oil and salt to the milk. Mix well till the sugar dissolves and add 1 cup flour and mix to a smooth paste.

4. Add the beaten egg and yeast. Mix well.

5. Add the flour and mix well till it forms smooth dough. Start with two cups of flour, and add extra a little at a time, till it forms soft non sticky dough. Knead well for 10 minutes. Cover and let it rest for 2-3 hours or till it doubles in volume.

6. Punch down the dough lightly. Divide it into small balls and flatten them into small circles. Fill them with 1 tablespoon of the filling.

7. Re-shape them back into small balls. Apply the egg wash.

8. Sprinkle the top with sesame seeds. Let it proof for another 20 minutes.

9. Bake them in a pre-heated oven at 180 degrees centigrade for 15-20 minutes.

BLT Macaroni Salad

 This summer salad is a fun take on a pasta salad. It combines the flavors of a BLT (bacon, lettuce, tomato) with creamy macaroni salad. It is packed with crispy bacon, tomatoes and crunchy green lettuce in addition to a tangy dressing. This is a great option to try when you are not in the mood for a lengthy cooking session.

Ingredients for the Salad

- Elbow macaroni (200 grams)
- Mayonnaise (1 cup)
- Greek or hung yoghurt (½ cup)
- Granulated sugar (1 tsp)
- Apple cider vinegar (1 tbsp)
- Garlic powder (1 tsp)
- Chilli flakes (½ tsp)
- Fresh dill (1 tsp)
- Black pepper (to taste)
- Onions (2, diced)
- Tomatoes (2, diced)
- Romaine lettuce (1 cup, diced)
- Bacon (200 grams, fried and crumbled)
- Salt to taste

Method

1. Cook the macaroni in salted water. Drain well.

2. Chop the onion, tomatoes, lettuce and bacon.

3. To prepare the dressing; in a large mixing bowl, whisk together mayonnaise, yoghurt, sugar, vinegar, garlic powder, chilli flakes, fresh dill, pepper and salt.

4. Add the cooked pasta to the dressing.

5. Stir in onions and tomatoes. Mix until evenly distributed. Cover and pop it into the fridge to chill.

6. Just before serving, add the lettuce and bacon. Mix well and serve. Store chilled.

Garlic Cheese Bread

 Usually when my better half Rajiv and I order pizza at home, we order in some garlic bread too. This bread is typically toasted with a garlic flavor and some olive oil, butter and herbs. It is a great starter and also goes well with pies and lasagna. This is a simple recipe of how garlic bread can be made at home.

Ingredients for the Dough

- Warm water (1/3 cup)
- Yeast (1 tsp)
- Sugar (1 tsp)
- Plain flour (1 cup)
- Milk powder (1 tbsp)
- Garlic (3 cloves, finely chopped)
- Unsalted butter (1 tsp, room temperature)
- Oregano (1 tsp)
- Salt (¼ tsp)
- Oil (1 tsp, to coat the dough)

Ingredients for the Filling

- Butter (¼ cup, melted)
- Garlic (3 cloves, finely chopped)
- Chilli flakes (2 tsp)
- Oregano or mixed herbs (1 tsp)
- Mozzarella cheese (½ cup)

Method

1. To make the dough, mix yeast and sugar in warm water and keep aside. Within a few minutes it should bubble up.

2. In a large mixing bowl, take plain flour, milk powder, minced garlic, oregano, butter and salt.

3. Add the activated yeast and knead the dough well for 5-8 minutes. The dough should be soft but not sticky. Add more milk or flour as needed. Coat the dough with oil, cover and let it rest for 2 hours.

4. After two hours punch the air out of the dough and roll it out into a circle.

5. In a small bowl, mix melted butter and minced garlic. Leave one inch around the perimeter of the dough and spread a generous dose of garlic butter into the centre.

6. Top one half (semi circle) of the dough with mozzarella cheese. Season with chilli flakes and oregano.

7. Fold the dough into a semi circle and seal the edges with wet fingers.

8. Brush generous amount of garlic butter over the dough. Sprinkle chilli flakes and oregano.

9. Make slice marks over the dough without cutting them fully.

10. Preheat the oven for at least 15 minutes, and then bake at 180 degrees centigrade for 20 minutes.

11. Cut the garlic bread into pieces and serve hot.

Note

- The water for activating the yeast should be warm to touch. If it is too hot, the yeast will die.
- You can also add other fillings such as sautéed mushrooms and corn.

Spring Roll

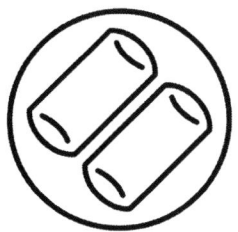 Fort Kochi has a special place in my heart. We often stroll around the quaint narrow streets of Jew Town along with our cousins. After one such outing, we reached back home tired and hungry. My aunt Vimala, who is a fabulous host had prepared a lovely tea party, with lots of snacks including these freshly fried spring rolls. It was the perfect way to end a wonderful day.

Ingredients for the Filling

- Cooked and shredded chicken (300 grams)
- Onions (2, diced)
- Ginger-garlic paste (1 tbsp)
- Green chilli (2, chopped)
- Carrot (1, diced)
- Beans (½ cup)
- Turmeric powder (¼ tsp)
- Black pepper powder (1 tsp)
- Garam masala (¼ tsp)
- Juice of ½ a lime
- Spring onion (½ cup)
- Celery (½ cup)
- Oil (2 tbsp)

Ingredients for the Batter

- Plain flour (1 cup)
- Egg (1)
- Salt (½ tsp)
- Water & milk (1¼ cup)
- Pepper powder (½ tsp)

Other Ingredients

- Egg (2, lightly beaten)
- Bread crumbs (2 cups)
- Oil for frying

Method

1. Heat oil in a pan and sauté the onions till it turns transparent.

2. Add the chopped chillies, ginger garlic paste, pepper powder, garam masala and sauté for 2 minutes.

3. Now add finely diced beans and carrots. After few minutes, add the cabbage and allow all the vegetables to get fully cooked.

4. Add shredded chicken, juice of half a lime, soya sauce, spring onion and chopped celery. Mix well. The filling should be dry. Remove the pan from the flame and let it cool.

5. To make the pancake batter, in a mixer, blend flour, egg, salt, pepper, milk and water. It should have a thin runny consistency with no lumps, but not too thin.

6. Heat a non-stick pan and make thin pancakes of about 8 inch diameter.

7. Once all the pancakes are done, place one pancake at a time on a flat surface and add 2 tablespoon of the chicken mix in the center. Carefully fold it into a cylindrical shape, making sure there are no holes or gaps. Use the batter to help stick the edges of the pancake.

8. Dip each piece into lightly beaten egg and coat with breadcrumbs to cover all sides. You can either freeze the rolls for future use or fry them right away.

9. Heat oil in a frying pan. When the oil is hot, reduce heat to medium flame and fry each roll till it turns golden brown on all sides.

10. Remove onto a paper towel lined plate to drain excess oil. Serve hot with tomato ketchup.

Mains

Fish Pie

 A fish pie is my favorite among all the pies there are! Possibly, this is because I have a preference for sea food. If you are like me and love sea food, you should surely give this a try. It has a layer of flaked fish, macaroni and vegetables in a creamy sauce topped with a golden toasted cheesy crust.

Ingredients for the Sauce

- Boneless fish (½ kg)
- Green chilli (3, chopped)
- Onion (2, sliced)
- Ginger garlic paste (2 tsp)
- Vinegar (1 tsp)
- Pepper (1 tsp)
- Salt to taste
- White sauce (2 cups, recipe no: 99)
- Egg (1)

Ingredients for the Filling

- Macaroni (2 cups)
- Carrot (½ cup, diced)
- Beans (½ cup, diced
- Button mushroom (2 cups, chopped)
- Butter (1 tbsp)
- Garlic (½ tsp)

Ingredients for the Topping

- Fresh bread crumbs (2-3 cups)
- Tomato (2, cut into thin round slices)
- Butter (1-2 tbsp)
- Grated cheese (1 cup)

Method

1. To flake the fish; cut the fish into pieces and cook in ¾ cup of water along with green chillies, sliced onions, ginger garlic paste, pepper, salt and vinegar.

2. Now take the cooked fish from the broth and flake it off the bones with your fingers and keep aside.

3. Take the remaining broth and blitz in the mixer. This will be used for the sauce.

4. Prepare the white sauce. To the sauce, add the prepared fish broth and mix well. Take off the fire and once it slightly cools down, add a beaten egg. Mix well till you get a silky creamy sauce and keep it aside.

5. Chop carrots, beans and mushrooms. Lightly sauté in butter with ½ teaspoon of garlic.

6. Cook the macaroni in salted water. Strain and keep aside.

7. Mix the cooked macaroni and sautéed vegetables along with half the quantity of sauce.

8. Grease the pie dish and assemble a layer of the mixed macaroni and flaked fish. Pour the remaining sauce over this and scatter a layer of fresh bread crumbs on top. Dot it with butter and arrange thinly sliced tomato over it. Sprinkle a generous layer of grated cheese on top.

9. Bake in a preheated oven at 180 degrees centigrade for 30 minutes or till the cheese melts and the crust turns brown. Serve warm with dinner rolls or garlic bread. Turn on the heat from the top of the oven in the last 10 minutes, to give the bread crumbs a golden hue.

Prawn Biryani

 This delectable dish is a family favorite that my mother makes so very well. It is so good, that I often prepare this for special occasions. It is a simple home style prawn biryani recipe that can be done in no time. The prawn is first cooked with spices, yoghurt and herbs and then layered with fragrant rice and caramelized onions.

Ingredients for the Masala

- Shelled and deveined prawns (500 grams)
- Ginger paste (1 tbsp)
- Garlic paste (1 tbsp)
- Green chilli (5)
- Turmeric powder (½ tsp)
- Salt (½ tsp)
- Oil and ghee (2 tbsp)
- Onions (4, sliced)
- Pepper powder (1½ tsp)
- Nutmeg powder (½ tsp)
- Garam masala powder (1 tsp)
- Tomato (2 large, diced)
- Fennel seed powder (1 tsp)

- Curd (2 tbsp)
- Juice of half a lime
- Coriander leaves and stems (a handful, finely chopped)
- Mint leaves (half cup, cut into small pieces)

Ingredients for the Rice

- Long grain basmati rice (3 cups)
- Ghee (2 tbsp)
- Cardamom (3)
- Mace (1)
- Bay leaf (1)
- Cinnamon (two inch stick)
- Cloves (3)
- Water (6 cups)
- Juice of 1 lime
- Onion (1 or 2, deep fried to crispy brown)
- Coriander leaves (a handful)
- Cashew nuts and raisins (fried to golden brown in a tablespoon of ghee)
- Salt to taste

Method

1. Make a paste of ginger, garlic and green chilli in the mixer.

2. Take 1½ teaspoon of this paste and marinate the prawns for 10 minutes along with some salt and turmeric powder. Cook this on a low flame in half a cup of water till the water gets fully absorbed and keep aside.

3. Heat oil and ghee in a kadai. Fry onions till slightly brown.

4. Add the remaining ginger-garlic-green chilli paste and cook till the raw smell goes. Add all the powders (pepper, nutmeg, garam masala) and fry lightly.

5. Add the diced tomato and cook till oil appears on top.

6. Now add the prawn mixture to this along with 1-2 tablespoon of thick curd. Add juice of half a lime.

7. Cook for 5 minutes on the low flame, stirring occasionally. Add a handful of finely chopped coriander leaves & stem. Mix well. The prawn masala should not be too dry or too watery.

8. To prepare the rice; wash and soak the rice in water for 30 minutes. Drain and keep aside.

9. Heat ghee and add the whole spices. Stir it around for a few seconds and add water.

10. When the water begins to boil; add rice, salt and lime juice. Let it cook until the water is evaporated. Fluff the rice with a fork.

11. To layer the biryani; first create a base of rice. Then add a layer of prawn masala, sprinkle fresh coriander leaves, crispy fried onion and few nuts and raisins.

12. Repeat the layering process and garnish with a generous dose of nuts, raisins and crispy fried onion. Add excess ghee if needed.

Note

- To make crispy fried onion, deep fry thinly sliced onions until golden brown and place them on a plate in a thin layer until cooled. It will turn crispy as it cools.

Whole Roast Chicken with Gravy

 Nothing beats a roasted chicken! This recipe is an Indian version with a spicy marinade. The skin is crispy and the chicken is nice and juicy. Make sure that you use the chicken with skin for the extra added flavor. (Psst! And don't forget to upload your Sunday roast on Instagram)

Ingredients for the Marination

- Whole chicken with skin (approx 1.2 kg)
- Butter (50 grams)
- Kashmiri chilli powder (2½ tbsp)
- Ginger garlic paste (3 tbsp)
- Pepper (½ tbsp)
- Cumin powder (1 tsp)
- Honey (2 tbsp)
- Vinegar (1½ tsp)
- Salt to taste

Additional Ingredients

- Lemon (1, halved)
- Potato (2 large, cut into big cubes)
- Carrot (1 cut into big round pieces)
- Onion (2 large, quartered)

- Corn flour (1 tsp)
- White wine (2 tbsp)
- Butter (1 tbsp)
- Plain flour (1 tsp)
- Chicken stock (1 cups)

Method

1. Make a marinade paste of all ingredients mentioned above for marination.

2. Clean the chicken well both inside and outside and pat dry with a paper towel.

3. Loosen the chicken skin using a blunt spoon. Be careful not to cut through the skin. If possible lightly score the chicken meat under the skin so that the marination can seep through.

4. Insert the marinade under the skin and gently massage it into all the corners under the skin.

5. Do the same on both sides of the chicken. Cover and keep it overnight in the fridge.

6. Remove the chicken from the fridge one hour before cooking so that it comes to room temperature.

7. Grease the roasting pan lightly with butter, place the vegetables sprinkled with salt on the base of the pan.

8. Place the lemon halves into the chicken cavity. Now place the chicken on the vegetables and tie the legs together with a twine.

9. Sprinkle some olive oil on top of the chicken so that the butter does not burn.

10. Roast in a pre heated oven at 220 degrees centigrade for the first 15 minutes. Then reduce the temperature to 180 degree centigrade for about 1 hour.

11. Spoon the pan gravy over the chicken at 30 minutes. If the top is getting too brown, cover it with an aluminum foil. You will know when that the chicken is fully cooked when the internal temperature reaches 165 degrees centigrade.

12. Once you remove the chicken from the oven, place it on a serving dish and arrange all the roasted vegetables around it.

13. To make the gravy; add wine and deglaze the roasting pan. Mix chicken broth and pan drippings. Melt butter over medium heat, add flour and stir for 1 minute. Mix the broth while whisking.

14. Continue cooking for 2 minutes, stirring regularly, until the gravy thickens. Season with salt and pepper to taste.

15. Pour this over the chicken or into each plate after serving the chicken and vegetables.

Note

- Allow the chicken to rest for 20 minutes before cutting.

Bhatoora

Bhatoora was an all time favorite dish when I was in college. We would often go to one of the local vegetarian restaurants for lunch and order this. Just the sight of the waiter bringing over the puffed-up football sized bhatoora was enough to make us drool. Having this with friends and then rushing back to college brings back fond memories of the days gone by. When paired with chickpea curry, the dish is called as *"channa bhatoora"*.

Ingredients

- Plain flour (3 cups)
- Instant dry yeast (1½ tsp)
- Sugar (2 tsp)
- Oil (3 tbsp)
- Curd (3 tbsp)
- Semolina or *rava* (4 tbsp)
- Lukewarm water (1 cup)
- Oil for frying
- Salt to taste

Method

1. In a large bowl, mix plain flour, semolina, salt, sugar and instant yeast.

2. Now add oil and curd and mix them.

3. Use warm water to knead the dough. Knead it for 5-7 minutes or until it becomes smooth and non sticky.

4. Grease a big bowl with oil. Place the dough into the bowl; apply some oil and cover it. Keep it in a warm place for one hour. The dough should double in size.

5. Knead the dough again and divide it into equal parts. Shape them into balls. Keep them rested for another 10-20 minutes.

6. Roll the dough ball into a 6-inch circle or oval shape. Make sure that you don't roll it out too thin. Keep the centers thick. Else when the bhatoora balloons up, the centre might crack open allowing oil to seep through.

7. Heat oil in a frying pan. Bhatoora should be fried in very hot oil. If the oil is not hot enough, the bhatoora will be greasy and will not puff up.

8. Place the rolled bhatoora into hot oil and press it with a spoon. It will puff up like a ball. Turn and cook until light golden brown in color from both the sides.

9. Take it out and place them on a paper towel. Enjoy them hot with pepper chicken curry or *channa masala*.

Home Style Chicken Biryani

 A visit to my godmother Annie aunty's home always leaves me in awe of the wonderful dishes that she prepares. The dining table will invariably be covered with yummy dishes from one end to the other, covering everything from soups and starters to desserts. My favourite however is her chicken biryani. It is simply loaded with flavor!

Ingredients

- Chicken (800 grams-1 kg)
- Basmati rice (3 cups, soaked for half hour)
- Ghee (2-3 tbsp)
- Cardamom (3)
- Cloves (2)
- Nutmeg flower (1)
- Bay leaf (1)
- Water (6 cups)
- Onions (5 sliced)
- Ginger garlic paste (2 tbsp)
- Green chilli (8-10, slit)
- Garam masala (1 tsp)
- Turmeric powder (½ tsp)
- Black pepper powder (1 tsp)

- Ripe tomato (3, diced)
- Curd (1-2 tbsp)
- Coriander leaves & stem (¾ cup, chopped)
- Mint leaves (1 cup, chopped)
- Cashew nuts (2 tbsp)
- Raisins (a handful)
- Salt to taste

Method

1. Marinate the chicken with salt, lime juice, ginger garlic paste, curd and pepper.

2. Heat 1 tablespoon of ghee in a large heavy bottomed vessel. Lightly fry the cardamom, cinnamon, cloves and nutmeg in the ghee.

3. Add the soaked and drained basmati rice and fry for a few minutes; but don't over mix and break the rice.

4. Add double the quantity of water to rice (6 cups water), 1 teaspoon ghee and salt to taste. Cook until the rice is done. Fluff it gently with a fork.

5. To make the chicken masala, fry 5 sliced onions until golden brown. Add the ginger garlic paste, green chilli and sauté.

6. Add the garam masala, turmeric and black pepper powder.

7. Once the onions mixture is nicely browned, add 3 diced ripe tomatoes. Let it simmer till the tomato is cooked well.

8. Now add the chicken and mix well. Cover and let it cook until the chicken is done.

9. When almost done, add 2 tablespoon of beaten curd to make it creamy.

10. Just before it is done, add a handful of coriander leaves and mint leaves.

11. In a frying pan, fry two thinly sliced onions in oil till golden and crispy. To make it crispy, you will need to take adequate quantity of oil.

12. Fry the cashew nuts and raisins in 1 tablespoon of ghee.

13. To assemble, layer the rice first. Then add some chicken masala, some fried onions, sprinkle cashew and raisins along with some of the ghee.

14. Repeat the layering till the dish is full, with about 2 or 3 layers. End with the rice, crispy fried onions, cashew and raisins on top.

15. Cover with an aluminum foil and bake this in the oven for 15 minutes, prior to serving.

Cauliflower Rice

For people on a low carbohydrate diet, this is the go to recipe! You can add or remove vegetables based on your preference. My husband Rajiv likes this dish as it goes well with some non-vegetarian curries. He made conscious efforts to cut down on carbohydrates and cauliflower rice was one option that really worked well for him as a replacement for rice.

Ingredients

- Cauliflower (250 grams)
- Onion (½, chopped)
- Tomato (1, chopped)
- Capsicum (½, chopped)
- Garlic (½ tsp)
- Garam masala (¼ tsp)
- Chilli powder (½ tsp)
- Turmeric powder (¼ tsp)

Method

1. Cut the cauliflower into small florets. Cauliflower is generally known to have small worms. So put it into salted, lukewarm water for at least half an hour so that that if there are any worms, it will rise to the top. Drain off the excess water by placing it in a colander.

2. Put the florets in a food processor and pulse until it is broken down into rice like pieces.

3. Heat oil in a large pan. Once the oil is hot, add onion and garlic and fry till the onions turn translucent. Add diced capsicum.

4. Now add chilli powder, garam masala powder and turmeric powder.

5. Once the raw flavor goes, add diced tomatoes and cook for a minute. Now add the cauliflower and cook for 3-4 minutes.

6. Add a table spoon of water. Cover the pan and cook the cauliflower rice on low heat for 4-5 minutes.

7. Top with coriander leaves and serve with *raita* or curries.

Keema Pav

 Peppery and flavorful, this is a quick recipe that is super appetizing. *Keema* is an Urdu word for minced meat. A colleague of mine adds *keema* into almost all his dishes and it makes everything so much tastier! As you can imagine, his office lunch box was always in full demand.

Ingredients

- Keema or mutton mince (350 grams, washed and drained)
- Oil (2-3 tbsp)
- Black peppercorn (6)
- Bay leaf (1 large)
- Cloves (2)
- Green cardamom (2)
- Cumin (1 tsp)
- Onions (2, medium minced)
- Ginger garlic paste (1 tbsp)
- Green chilli (3)
- Tomato (2, pureed)
- Green peas (½ cup)
- Turmeric powder (¼ tsp)
- Chilli powder (1 tsp)
- Cumin powder (1 tbsp)

- Garam masala powder (1 tsp)
- Coriander and mint (freshly chopped)
- *Kasuri methi* or fenugreek (2 tbsp)
- Pan roasted potatoes (1 cup, optional)
- Ghee (1 tbsp)
- Salt to taste

Method

1. Heat oil in a kadai and add the whole spices – pepper corn, cloves, cardamom, bay leaf and cumin.

2. Add the finely minced onions, ginger garlic paste and green chilli.

3. When the raw smell goes, add turmeric powder, chilli powder, coriander powder and cumin powder. Sauté lightly.

4. Add pureed tomato, green peas and cook on medium flame.

5. Once the masala comes together, add the *keema*. Mix well. Add salt and a splash of water. Cover and cook till the meat is done.

6. Add crushed *kasuri methi* and garam masala. Add pan roasted potatoes.

7. Pour 1 tablespoon ghee and a handful of chopped coriander and mint leaves. Serve hot with buttered and pan toasted *pav*.

Chicken & Mushroom Quiche

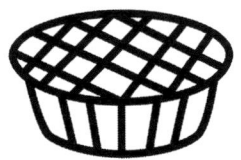 A Christmas spread is never complete without a quiche! This dish has a flaky pie crust with a creamy chicken, mushroom and peas filling. My aunty Laila has a great collection of recipes and this is one of her quick and easy dishes. If you are in the mood for a something tasty, you don't need to wait for Christmas to try it.

Ingredients for the Pie Base

- Plain flour (200 grams)
- Cold butter (100 grams, cubed)
- Egg (1, lightly beaten)
- Salt to taste

Ingredients for the Filling

- Chicken (1 cup, cooked & shredded)
- Mushroom (½ cup, sautéed in butter)
- Peas (½ cup, cooked)
- Shallots/onion (¼ cup, chopped)
- Fresh cream (1 cup)
- Eggs (2, beaten)
- Mozzarella or parmesan cheese (1 cup, grated)
- Pepper
- Salt and mixed herbs to taste

Method

1. Combine the butter, flour and salt. Rub them between your fingers to form a crumbly mix. Don't over mix, as the heat from our hands can melt the butter.

2. Add the beaten egg and form smooth dough. Roll this out into an even circle and line a round 7" pie dish with the pastry.

3. Remove the excess from the edge of the pan. Keep it aside in a refrigerator.

4. Beat the eggs and fresh cream in a bowl. Add salt, pepper and mixed herbs.

5. Heat butter in a pan, add garlic and shallots. When it turns translucent, add mushrooms and green peas. Sauté till they are cooked. Add the shredded chicken and remove from heat.

6. Pour the egg mix onto the pie base and sprinkle the cooked chicken, mushroom, peas and shallots.

7. Next, spread a cup of grated cheese over it & bake in a preheated oven at 180 degrees centigrade for 20-25 minutes or until crisp & golden. Serve warm.

Pesaha Appam

 The *Pesaha appam* is a rice cake that is derived from the ancient Jewish tradition. The bread is prepared without yeast in accordance with the commemoration of *Pesaha* or Passover in the Old Testament. This unleavened bread is also called as *Inriyappam* or *Kurisappam* and is made by the Catholic community in Kerala. It is served on the night of Maundy Thursday to commemorate the last supper of Jesus Christ.

Ingredients for the Appam

- *Urad dal* (¼ cup, soaked for 2 hours)
- Grated coconut (¼ cup)
- Shallots (2)
- Garlic (2 flakes)
- Cumin seeds (1 pinch)
- Rice powder (2 tbsp)
- A pinch of salt
- Water

Ingredients for the Jaggery Milk

- Rice powder (1 tbsp)
- Thin coconut milk / 2ⁿᵈ extract (1 cup)
- Thick Coconut milk / 1ˢᵗ extract (1 cup)
- Jaggery (1 cup)
- A pinch of ginger powder
- A pinch of salt

Method

1. In a mixer, grind all the *appam* ingredients into a fine smooth batter. Let it rest for half an hour.

2. Coat a 5 or 6 inch steel flat round dish with sufficient ghee and pour the batter.

3. Place the palm leaves in the shape of a cross on top of the *appam* and steam for 15 minutes.

4. For the jaggery milk, boil the rice powder with second extract of coconut milk.

5. Pour jaggery. Add ginger powder (*chukku*), salt and thick coconut milk.

6. As the milk thickens remove from heat.

7. Chill and serve along with the *Pesaha Appam*.

Moussaka

 *Moussaka* is a Greek version of the Italian lasagna. It is made with layers of eggplant, potato, meat sauce and topped with a white sauce and cheese that crisps up and becomes golden brown in the oven. While *moussaka* can be time-consuming to prepare, it is surely worth the effort. My sister recently shared this recipe along with the photo of the dish. Ten minutes later came another picture of a clean dish; as the moussaka was polished off by the kids instantly.

Ingredients

- Eggplants (2-3 large)
- Potatoes (3)
- Onion (1, large)
- Garlic (1 tsp)
- Minced beef (500 grams)
- Egg yolks (2)
- Vegetable oil for frying
- Salt (1 tsp)
- White sauce (Recipe no: 99)
- Marinara sauce (Recipe no: 98)

Method

1. Slice the whole eggplants into flat slices of 1cm thickness. Season with salt and set aside for 30 minutes. Then pat it dry with a paper towel.

2. Peel the potatoes and slice them into flat slices.

3. Heat oil in a pan and fry the eggplants and potatoes until golden. Transfer to a paper towel to get rid of excess oil.

4. To prepare the meat sauce, heat oil in a pan and cook the minced meat until brown. Add the marinara sauce and get it to a thick meat sauce consistency.

5. Prepare white sauce. Add the egg yolks and whisk until smooth.

6. Add 4-5 tablespoons of the white sauce to the meat mixture and mix.

7. Finally to assemble the moussaka; take a deep pie dish. Layer the potatoes in an ovenproof dish. Then layer half of the eggplants.

8. Pour the meat mixture and spread evenly. Add a thin layer of white sauce. Repeat the layering and finish off with a thick layer of white sauce on top. Grate some cheese over it.

9. Bake in a preheated oven for 40-50 minutes or until golden brown. Remove from the oven and let it cool for at least 30 minutes before cutting.

Spaghetti & Meat Balls

 Spaghetti and meatball is a classic combo that is popular all over the world! This is an Italian-American dish consisting of spaghetti, tomato sauce and meatballs. The meatballs are gently fried and then cooked in a creamy tomato sauce. If prepped in advance they can be made in no time.

Ingredients for the Meatballs

- Minced beef (500 grams)
- Egg (1)
- Freshly grated cheese (2 tbsp)
- Garlic (1 tsp, minced)
- Dried oregano (1 tsp)
- Onion (1, minced)
- Coriander leaves (2 tbsp, finely chopped)
- Breadcrumbs (3 tbsp or enough for binding)
- Ground black pepper (1 tsp)
- Red chilli flakes (1 tsp)
- Salt to taste

Other Ingredients

- Marinara sauce (Recipe no: 98)
- Cream or full fat milk (50 ml)
- Parmesan or mozzarella cheese (½-¾ cup, grated)
- Pepper powder (1 tsp)
- Salt to taste

Method

1. To make the meatballs; put all the ingredients into a large bowl and then using your hands mix and shape into small balls. Don't over mix. Place the meatballs in the freezer for 10 minutes.

2. Shallow fry the meatballs in olive oil till it turns brown and is cooked through.

3. Prepare the Marinara sauce. To the sauce add the cream and then drop the meatballs in one by one. Don't stir the meat balls too much, as you don't want to break them up.

4. Add grated cheese.

5. Cook everything for about 15 minutes. At the end of cooking time, check the seasoning, as you may want more salt or pepper.

6. Serve on top of freshly cooked spaghetti.

Palappam

 A classic Kerala breakfast menu will always feature the ever famous *appam*. For a long time I stayed away from making this as I always construed it to be a complicated affair. But ever since I came across this easy *palappam* recipe it has been a permanent addition to our weekly breakfast menu.

Ingredients

- Raw rice (2 cups)
- *Urad dal* (2 tbsp)
- Grated coconut (1 cup)
- Cooked rice (1 tbsp)
- Instant yeast (¼ tsp)
- Salt
- Sugar (1 tbsp)
- Water as required (approx 1½ cups)

Method

1. In a bowl, soak the raw rice and *urad dal* for 4 – 5 hours.

2. In a mixer, grind together raw rice, *urad dal*, grated coconut, cooked rice and instant yeast. Use cold water while grinding. You may need to do this in 2 batches in the mixer.

3. Add salt and sugar. Mix well and allow it to ferment for 6-7 hours or overnight.

4. Pour the batter into an *appam chatti*. Rotate the pan once to get crisp lacy *appam*.

Bacon & Egg Fried Rice

 What makes this fried rice dish extra special is that the rice and vegetables are fried in bacon fat. So the whole dish has a smoky yummy bacon flavor to it. My sister often makes this for the kids' lunch box.

Ingredients

- Basmati rice (2 cups)
- Oil (1 tsp)
- Bacon (6 to 7 strips)
- Carrot (1 cup, small cubes)
- Green peas (½ cup)
- Cabbage (2 cups, thinly chopped)
- Egg (3)
- Pepper (1½ tsp)
- Soya sauce (2 tbsp)
- Salt (½ tsp)

Method

1. Wash the basmati rice and cook it in sufficient water. Add salt and a teaspoon of oil while cooking. Let it boil for 5 minutes. Turn off the heat and strain the water.

2. Fluff the rice with a fork so that the rice does not stick together. Keep it aside and let it cool.

3. In a wok or deep frying pan, cut the bacon strips into to 1 inch pieces and fry it. The fat will ooze out of the bacon. Transfer the bacon pieces into another dish.

4. Into the same pan, add the carrots, green peas and the cabbage. Mix well, cover the pan and let it cook on low heat for 5 minutes.

5. Once the vegetables are done, keep the heat on high. Add 3 to 4 beaten eggs and scramble it well. Now remove the egg-vegetable mixture and keep aside.

6. In the same wok, add 1 tablespoon oil, add half of the prepared rice, half of the egg-vegetable mix, soya sauce and pepper. Mix well.

7. Repeat the same with the rest of the rice, vegetables and sauces. This is so that it becomes easier to mix the rice, sauces and vegetables.

8. Garnish with spring onion and serve with chilli chicken

Macaroni Shepherds' Pie

 This delicious dish combines two classics – Macaroni n Cheese and Shepherd's Pie to make one mouth watering meal. Mac 'n' cheese is one of world's most popular comfort foods. Shepherds' pie has a layer of meat and vegetables cooked in a savory sauce and topped with creamy mashed potatoes. I personally really like this dish and can have it anytime!

Ingredients for the Pie

- Elbow macaroni (250 grams)
- Minced meat (300 grams)
- Potato (2 large peeled, boiled with salt and mashed well)
- Grated cheese
- Tomato (1, cut into round thin slices)
- Salt (as required)
- White sauce (2 cups, recipe no: 99)
- Marinara sauce (2 cups, recipe no: 98)

Method

1. In a large pot of boiling water, cook macaroni with 1 teaspoon salt and 1 teaspoon oil. Turn off the heat when the macaroni is al dente (still firm). Drain and keep aside.

2. Prepare white sauce.

3. Add the cooked macaroni into the white sauce and keep aside.

4. Prepare the marinara sauce. Brown minced meat in a frying pan and add the marinara sauce. Adjust consistency to get a semi-dry thick meat sauce.

5. Grease a baking dish. To assemble the pie, first place macaroni and white sauce at the bottom of the dish. Then layer the minced meat sauce on top. Repeat the layering.

6. Place the mashed potato on top to cover the pie. Decorate with round sliced tomato and a generous dose of grated cheese.

7. Bake in a preheated oven for 20 to 25 minutes.

8. In the last 5 minutes, turn on the heat from the top of the oven (broil) so that the cheese melts.

Kappa Puzhukku (Tapioca)

 This dish is a specialty of my house help, Sarasamma. The kappa which is subtle in flavor with tangy fish curry is an absolute winning combination. My husband Rajiv is a huge fan of this style of kappa preparation. The fun is in mixing the kappa and fish curry together to create a flavorful mish mash.

Ingredients for the Kappa

- Tapioca (1kg, cubed)
- Water
- Turmeric (1 pinch)
- Salt (½ tsp)

Ingredients to Grind

- Coconut (¾ cup, grated)
- Cumin seeds (¼ tsp)
- Garlic (2 cloves, chopped)
- Green chilli (1 or 2)
- Turmeric powder (¼ tsp)

Ingredients for the Tempering

- Coconut oil (2 tbsp)
- Mustard seeds (1 tsp)
- Small onions (3, chopped)
- Red dry whole chilli (3)
- Curry leaves (1 sprig)

Method

1. Peel off the skin from the tapioca, cut into cubes and wash under running water. Put the tapioca in the pressure cooker, along with water, salt, turmeric powder and cook until 1 whistle.

2. Check if it is soft and fork-tender. Depending on the type of kappa, it may sometimes take longer.

3. Drain the water from the cooked tapiocas and keep aside.

4. In a mixer, pulse the "to grind ingredients" to a coarse paste.

5. In a pan, add the tapioca and the ground coconut paste and cook for a minute.

6. Pour half cup of water. Add 1 teaspoon salt and combine well. Gently mash the tapioca.

7. Let it cook for 10 minutes on low heat until the gravy is absorbed. Remove the pan from the heat and keep aside covered.

8. To temper, heat oil in a pan and splutter mustard seeds. Add shallots, dry red chilli and curry leaves. Sauté till the shallots turn brown.

9. Pour this tempering over the cooked tapioca. Serve warm along with fish curry.

Instant Kallappam

 I am always on the lookout for easy instant recipes. This recipe was shared by my aunt Singamma and is a favourite among many of my relatives. It is a healthy breakfast option as it contains no oil. It can be eaten with a meat based curry such as pork or mutton.

Ingredients

- Rice powder (1 cup)
- *Rava*/semolina (1 cup)
- Cooked rice (1 cup)
- Yeast (½ tsp)
- Sugar (4 tsp)
- Salt (½ tsp)
- Water

Method

1. In a mixer, grind the rice powder, *rava,* cooked rice, sugar, salt, yeast and water to get a fine batter. It should have the consistency of idly batter.

2. Pour the batter into a container and allow it to ferment for 1-2 hours.

3. Pour one ladle onto a greased cast iron *tava* and cook covered on low flame.

4. Serve hot with pork or mutton curry.

Creamy Spinach Pasta

 For an occasional indulgent meal, this creamy spinach pasta is a great option for you to try. This dish requires only a few ingredients, cooks super fast and leaves you feeling full and happy! This is a vegetarian's delight and everyone will love it. The added bonus is that spinach is a super food as it is loaded with tons of nutrients.

Ingredients

- Pasta (2 cups, uncooked)
- Oil (1 tsp)
- Salt (1 tsp)
- Olive oil (1-2 tbsp)
- Onion (1 large, chopped)
- Garlic paste (½ tsp)
- Spinach leaves without stem (2-3 cups, chopped)
- White Sauce (2 cups, recipe no: 99)
- Red chilli flakes (1 tsp)

Method

1. Bring a large pot of water to boil, add salt and a few drops of oil. After the water boils add the pasta. Cook the pasta until it is tender. This will take about 10 minutes. Drain the water and set the pasta aside.

2. Prepare white sauce using cream.

3. In another pan, sauté onion and garlic. Once the onions have softened, add the spinach leaves.

4. When the spinach has wilted, turn off the heat. Add the spinach to white sauce. Add chilli flakes. Mix well. Pour the sauce over pasta and toss.

5. Serve the pasta hot with toasted garlic bread.

Lasagna

 One of Garfield's favourite dishes, lasagna is rich and creamy with several layers of flat pasta, sauces, meats and cheese. What goes into 'authentic lasagna' is often highly debatable. My version is made of ingredients that are easily available in India. I have used store bought pasta sheets for this recipe. Like Garfield says "you just can't go wrong with the world's most perfect food!"

Ingredients

- Lasagna sheets
- Minced meat (300 grams)
- Mozzarella (1 cup, for topping)
- Salt (½ tsp)
- White sauce (2 cups, recipe no: 99)
- Marinara sauce (2 cups, recipe no: 98)

Method

1. Brown the minced meat in a frying pan. Add the marinara sauce and cook till you get a thick meat sauce.

2. Prepare the white sauce.

3. Meanwhile, cook the lasagna noodle in salted water.

4. Lightly grease a deep 9x13 inch pan. To assemble, spread about 1 cup of meat sauce at the bottom of the prepared pan. Place the lasagna sheets on top. Spread a third of the white sauce mixture. Top with cheese.

5. Repeat the layers and top with remaining cheese. Cover loosely with aluminum foil.

6. Bake in a preheated oven at 180 degrees centigrade for 25-30 minutes. Serve hot.

Kerala Style Mutton Biryani

 This flavor packed biryani is layered with rice, mutton masala, crispy fried onions and fresh herbs. It can seem elaborate to prepare this dish at home, but the efforts are well worth the results! Use goat meat from the leg or shoulder for this awesome preparation.

Ingredients for the Mutton Marinade

- Goat meat (1 kg)
- Pepper (1 tsp)
- Fennel seed powder (1 tsp)
- Turmeric powder (½ tsp)
- Yogurt (½ cup)
- Salt (1 tsp)

Ingredients for the Mutton Masala

- Onions (4, sliced)
- Ginger (3 inch long piece, minced)
- Garlic cloves (7 minced)
- Spicy green chillies (7, minced)
- Tomatoes (3, medium chopped)
- Turmeric powder (½ tsp)

- Coriander powder (2 tbsp)
- Garam masala powder (2 tsp)
- Black pepper (1 tsp)
- Fresh coriander leaves (½ cup)
- Fresh mint leaves (¼ cup)
- Salt (½ tsp)

Ingredients for the Garnish

- Onions (3, medium sliced)
- Raisins (⅓ cup)
- Raw cashews (⅓ cup)
- Fresh coriander (½ cup, chopped)
- Fresh mint leaves (½ cup, chopped)
- Fresh pineapple (¼ cup, chopped, optional)

Ingredients for the Rice

- Basmati rice (3 cups)
- Water (6 cups)
- Cinnamon (2 sticks)
- Cloves (6)
- Cardamom (6)

Method

1. Heat 2 tablespoon ghee in a heavy bottomed pan. Fry cashew nuts until light brown. Transfer to a bowl. Add golden raisins and fry till it plums up. Keep the fried cashew nuts and raisins aside. Keep the ghee aside for using later.

2. In a heavy bottomed kadai, heat 1 cup oil. Add thinly sliced onions and fry until it turns golden brown. This will take about 20-25 minutes. Transfer the browned onions onto a plate and spread it in a thin layer. It will crisp up as it cools down.

3. Into the same oil, add 3 onions and sauté. Add ginger, garlic and green chilli. Add turmeric powder and salt. Mix well.

4. Add 3 diced tomato, coriander leaves and mint leaves. Mix well and sauté for 10 minutes.

5. Now add coriander powder, garam masala and pepper powder. Sauté until the raw smell goes.

6. Add the mutton and mix well. Add half cup water. Cover and let it cook until the meat is almost done.

7. Crush the crisp golden brown onions with your hands and add that to the mutton masala. Mix well. Turn off the heat when the meat is fully done.

8. In the mean time; wash, soak and drain the rice. In a saucepan take 6 cups of water. Add cardamom and cloves. Allow it to come to a boil.

9. In a heavy bottomed pan, heat 2 tablespoon ghee and fry the rice for about 6 to 7 minutes. Mix gently so that the rice does not break.

10. Add the boiled water along with the whole spices. Add salt and lime juice. Cover and let the rice cook until it is done.

11. To assemble the biryani; first place one layer of mutton, followed by rice. Drizzle 1 tablespoon of ghee, a pinch of garam masala and pineapple pieces.

12. Add fried cashew nuts and raisins. Top with mint leaves, coriander leaves and fried onion. Repeat the layering.

13. Drizzle 2 tablespoon of saffron mixed in hot milk over the rice.

14. Cover the dish with aluminum foil. Bake at 180 degrees centigrade for 20 minutes.

15. Serve hot with *raita*, pickle and *papadam*.

Pav Bhaji

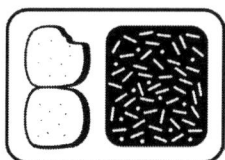 Pav Bhaji is a much loved Indian street food. My college had a great Pav Bhaji counter by the basketball court. The chef would simultaneously and very skillfully whip up the dish for multiple people on the super sized *tava*. The *bhaji masala* is topped with a dollop of butter, diced onions and served with a lemon wedge and butter toasted *Pav*. This recipe is my attempt in recreating those delightful flavors from my college days.

Ingredients to Pressure Cook

- Cauliflower florets (1 cup, cut into small pieces)
- Capsicum (½ cup, chopped)
- Carrot (1 cup, chopped)
- Green peas (½ cup)
- Potato (½ cup, peeled and chopped)
- Beetroot (¼ cup, cubed)
- Green chilli (2, chopped)
- Water (1 cup)
- Salt to taste

Other Ingredients

- Tomato (1 cup, chopped)
- Butter (6 tbsp)
- Onion (1 cup, chopped)
- Garlic paste (1 tsp)
- Kashmiri red chilli powder (1 tsp)
- Pav bhaji masala (1 tsp)
- Garam masala (1 tsp)
- Grated paneer (½ cup, optional)
- Lemon juice (1 tbsp)
- Fresh coriander (½ cup, chopped)
- *Kasuri methi* leaves or dry fenugreek leaves (1 tsp)
- Salt to taste

Method

1. Pressure cook the vegetables with salt and turmeric powder for two whistles. Remove from heat.

2. Heat butter in a pan. Add onion, garlic paste and fry till the onion turns translucent.

3. Now add red chilli powder, pav bhaji masala and garam masala and cook for a minute.

4. Add the cooked vegetables in the pan along with the water remaining in the cooker and mix well.

5. Mash the vegetable mix using a potato masher till it is mushy and mixed very well.

6. Keep adding a little hot water to the bhaji and cook until it thickens, for 10-12 minutes on medium low heat.

7. Add grated paneer, lemon juice, salt, coriander leaves, *Kasuri methi* and mix well.

8. Garnish with a generous dollop of butter, chopped onions and a squeeze of lime.

9. Serve with lightly buttered and pan toasted *pav*. Don't skip the garnish as that is what gives it the street style zing!

Note

- If you don't have pav bhaji masala, add ½ tsp of coriander powder, ½ tsp of cumin seed powder and ¼ tsp pepper powder.

Sides & Curries

Pork Vindaloo

 Pork vindaloo is an amazing Goan dish of Portuguese origin. It is rich and tangy with a hint of sweetness. If you have all the ingredients, it is an easy dish to prepare. Make sure that you use pork which is a mix of fat and meat pieces as the fat will render and add to the flavor. This dish matures and tastes better the next day and goes very well with appams.

Ingredients for the Pork

- Pork (1 kg, boneless, 2 inch cubed pieces)
- White vinegar (4-5 tbsp)
- Onions (4)
- Garlic (2 pods)
- Ginger (3 inch piece)
- Green chilli (2)
- Tomato (2)
- Oil
- Salt to taste
- Sugar (½ tsp)

Ingredients for the Paste

- Kashmiri chilli powder (3 tbsp)
- Turmeric powder (1 tsp)
- Coriander powder (2 tbsp)
- Pepper powder (1 tsp)
- Garam masala (1 ½ tsp)
- Fenugreek powder (¼ tsp)
- Mustard seed powder (1½ tsp)
- Cumin seed powder (½ tsp)
- Fennel seed powder (1 tsp)

Method

1. Wash the pork with vinegar and salt. Keep it aside after draining the water.
2. In a pressure cooker, add 4 table spoons of oil.
3. Sautee the onions, ginger, garlic, green chilli till the onions becomes light brown in color.
4. In a small bowl, make a paste out of the chilli powder, turmeric powder, coriander powder, pepper powder, garam masala, mustard seed powder, cumin seeds powder, fennel seed powder and fenugreek powder in ¼ cup of vinegar.
5. Add this paste to the pressure cooker and let it simmer.
6. Add the tomatoes and let it cook till the tomatoes become soft.

7. Add the pork along with two table spoon of vinegar and let it cook for 2-3 whistles or until the pork is done.

8. Once the meat is soft, add more vinegar if required and half a tea spoon of sugar. Let it cook for some more time, till the vindaloo turns into a thick syrupy consistency.

9. Serve hot with rice or appams. The flavor will get enhanced as it sits for longer.

Note

- Instead of using masala powders for the paste, you can use whole spices. As an alternate for chilli powder, use 20 Kashmiri chillies. Soak the chilli and whole spices in vinegar for 30 minutes and then grind them to a paste.

Butter Chicken

 This was a recipe that my mom learnt when she went for a cooking class many years back at the Lotus Club, Cochin. This restaurant style butter chicken is simply mouth watering. This curry goes very well with *tandoori rotis, naans* and *kulchas*. It is no wonder that the Punjabis swear by this dish. It is probably one of the most ordered dishes in all the *dhabas* that we have dotting our national highways.

Ingredients for Marination

- Chicken (500 grams)
- Ginger garlic paste (1 tbsp)
- Turmeric powder (½ tsp)
- Chilli powder (½ tbsp)
- Curd (2 tbsp)
- Salt (½ tsp)

Ingredients for the Masala

- Oil (3 tbsp)
- Big onions (2 sliced)
- Garlic paste (1 tbsp)
- Ginger paste (1 tsp)
- Garam masala (½ tsp)
- Kashmiri chilli powder (2 tbsp)

- Kasuri methi (1 tsp)

- Ripe red tomatoes (4)

- Cashew nuts (4 tbsp, soaked in hot water)

- Butter (50 grams)

- Tomato ketchup (2 tbsp)

- Fresh cream (½ cup)

Method

1. Marinate the chicken and set aside for 30 minutes-1 hour.

2. In a large pan, shallow fry the chicken until half cooked, for about 2-3 minutes on each side. Remove the chicken from the oil.

3. In the same pan, sauté onion and ginger garlic paste. Fry till the onions turn light brown.

4. Add Kashmiri chilli powder, garam masala and half teaspoon *kasuri methi*. Add chopped tomato and cashew nuts and continue to cook for around 10 minutes.

5. Turn off the heat and let it cool down. Grind this to a paste. You can also use a hand blender to make a puree.

6. Add butter and let it cook again. Add the half fried chicken pieces back to the pan. Cover and cook for 15 minutes.

7. When the chicken is cooked add the fresh cream, tomato ketchup and the remaining *kasuri methi* and simmer till the oil separates and the chicken is fully cooked.

8. Serve hot with *roti, appams, naans* or plain rice.

Meen Curry in Coconut Milk

 Meen curry is synonymous with the Kerala cuisine. Kerala has a long coastline that is also interspersed with back waters and canals throughout the landscape. Hence fish curry is a staple dish in Kerala. This is a simple Thrissur style of preparation where the spices and fish are cooked in coconut milk. Ensure that you use fresh fish when you make this dish.

Ingredients for the Meen Curry

- Kingfish (½ kg, curry pieces)
- Shallots (12 or ½ cup, sliced)
- Garlic (8 cloves, sliced)
- Ginger (1 inch, sliced)
- Green chilli (3, slit)
- Chilli powder (2½ tsp)
- Turmeric powder (½ tsp)
- Curry leaves (1 sprig)
- Salt to taste
- Coconut oil (2 tbsp)
- *Kodampulli* (2
- First extract of coconut milk (1 cup)
- Second extract of coconut milk (2 cups)

Ingredients for Tempering

- Coconut oil (1 tbsp)

- Red chilli powder (½ tsp)

- Shallots (5, sliced)

- Curry leaves (1 sprig)

Method

1. Soak the *kodampulli* in 1 cup hot water for 15 minutes.

2. In a mud pot or kadai, add coconut oil, shallots, garlic, ginger, green chilli, chilli powder, turmeric powder, curry leaves and salt. Use your hand to mix and crush the mixture for 1 minute.

3. Pour the second extract of coconut milk, turn on the heat and add the fish pieces and *kodampulli* along with the water it was soaked in. Cook until the fish is done.

4. Add thick coconut milk / first extract and rotate the pan. Cook on a low flame for two more minutes. Remove from fire.

5. For tempering, heat coconut oil in a small pan, add shallots and fry until golden brown. Add curry leaves and red chilli powder. Pour this over the meen curry. The curry should be rested for some time to help the flavors settle.

Note

- For sourness, you can use *kodampulli,* raw mango or tomato.

- I use a mix of Kashmiri chilli powder and spicy chilli powder for this recipe.

Paneer Lababdar

Paneer lababdar is a rich combination of cottage cheese and exotic gravy made from tomato puree, chopped onions, cashew nuts and spices. This dish has a lovely tang to it and is full of aromas. When we add honey and cream to this mix, we get a faintly sweet taste which makes it super lip-smacking. This curry goes very well with *roti* or *naan*.

Ingredients for the Paneer

- Paneer cubes (200 grams)
- Grated paneer (50 grams)
- Oil (2 tbsp)
- Cumin seeds (1 tsp)
- Green cardamoms (2)
- Cloves (2)
- Onions (3, medium chopped)
- Tomatoes (3, medium chopped)
- Cashew nuts (8-10)
- Salt to taste

Ingredients for the Gravy

- Oil (1 tbsp)
- Butter (2 tsp)
- Garlic (1 tbsp, finely chopped)
- Ginger (½ tbsp, finely chopped)
- Green chilli (1, chopped)
- Kashmiri chilli powder (1 tsp)
- Dry fenugreek leaves or *kasuri methi* (½ tsp)
- Honey (1 tsp)
- Garam masala powder (¼ tsp)
- Chopped fresh coriander leaves (2 tbsp)
- Fresh cream (2 tbsp, for drizzling)
- Fresh coriander (for garnish)

Method

1. Heat oil in a *kadai*; add cumin seeds, green cardamoms, cloves and sauté till the mix turns fragrant.
2. Add onions and sauté till golden brown. Add tomatoes and mix.
3. Add salt, cashew nuts and sauté for 4 to 5 minutes or till the tomatoes are soft and pulpy.
4. Take the *kadai* off the heat and allow the mixture to cool slightly.
5. Add half cup water and using a hand blender make a puree out of this mix.

6. To make the tempering, heat oil and butter in the same *kadai*. Add garlic, ginger and green chilli and sauté for 2 minutes.

7. Add Kashmiri chilli powder and mix. Add the ground paste and stir for 1-2 minutes. Add 1½ cups of hot water and bring the mix to a boil.

8. Add dry fenugreek leaves powder and honey and mix. Add grated paneer and mix well.

9. Add the paneer cubes, adjust salt, add garam masala powder and coriander leaves and gently mix.

10. Add fresh cream, mix and take the *kadai* off the heat.

11. Transfer this mixture into a serving bowl and drizzle fresh cream on top and garnish with coriander sprig.

Chicken in Creamy Mushroom Sauce

 Some time ago, my husband Rajiv declared that he was tired of the usual chicken curry that I prepare and that I should try out something new every week (eye roll). So, I happened to experiment with this dish and it turned out fabulous! It goes very well with garlic bread or pasta.

Ingredients

- Cashew nuts (1/3 cup, soaked in water for half an hour)
- Chicken breast (300 grams, cut into strips)
- Olive oil (2 tbsp)
- Garlic (4-5 cloves, minced)
- Shallot (8, finely chopped)
- Button mushrooms (150 to 200 grams, finely sliced)
- White wine (½ cup)
- Chicken stock (1½ cups)
- Worcester sauce (2 tbsp)
- Dried thyme (1 tsp)
- Grated nutmeg (one pinch)
- Salt & pepper (to season chicken, and later, the sauce)

Method

1. Place the cashew nuts in the blender, add ¼ cup of chicken stock/water and blend until you get a thick, creamy texture.

2. Season the chicken breasts with salt and pepper. In a pan, heat olive oil and add minced garlic and cook for about 30 seconds.

3. Add the chicken strips and cook until they are browned on either side. Once the chicken is brown; place them on a separate plate and let the chicken rest.

4. Heat a tablespoon of olive oil in the same pan and add a chopped shallot and let it caramelize. Add the remaining minced garlic & cook for about 30 seconds.

5. Add the sliced mushrooms to the pan & cook until the water dries up.

6. Take the pan off the heat momentarily & add half cup of wine & put the pan back on heat. Cook until the wine has reduced by half.

7. Add the remaining chicken stock & cook until it has reduced slightly.

8. Add the thyme, grated nutmeg & Worcester sauce and stir to combine.

9. Now add the chicken pieces back to the pan followed by the cashew cream & let it cook on a low simmer for a couple of minutes.

10. Season with salt & pepper. Serve with garlic bread or with pasta.

Beef Ularthiyathu

 Of all the beef preparations in the world, I don't think that anything would beat the Kerala style beef *ularthiyathu* also known as the Kerala beef dry fry. The beef is slow roasted with the spices, coconut oil, curry leaves and crispy coconut bits. It is no wonder that it is the best known dish from Kerala. It goes fantastically well with the world famous Kerala *parotta*!

Ingredients for Marination

- Cubed beef (1 kg)
- Ginger paste (1 heaped tbsp)
- Garlic paste (1 heaped tbsp)
- Green chilli (4, slit)
- Coriander powder (1 heated tbsp)
- Turmeric powder (1 tsp)
- Pepper powder (1 tsp)
- Garam masala (1 tsp)
- Vinegar (1 tbsp)
- Salt (2 tsp)
- Coconut slices (½ cup)

Ingredients for Frying

- Onions (3, sliced)
- Chilli powder (2 tsp)
- Pepper powder (1 tsp)
- Garam masala (1 tsp)
- Oil (5-6 tbsp)
- Curry leaves (2 sprigs)

Method

1. Marinate the beef with ginger garlic paste, green chilli, coriander powder, turmeric powder, pepper powder, coconut bits, garam masala, vinegar and salt. Massage them well into the raw beef and keep it aside for half an hour.

2. Pressure cook the beef mixture till it is ¾th cooked. This would need about 3 whistles. There is no need to add water as the water will get released from the meat. By the end it, there should be very little or no water remaining in the cooker.

3. Heat sufficient oil in a kadai and add 2 large onions and 2 sprigs of curry leaves. Sauté until the onions turn brown.

4. Over low heat add chilli powder, pepper powder and garam masala powder.

5. Now add the beef with the stock remaining in the cooker and let it get coated with all the masalas.

6. Sauté and fry till the beef is completely dry. Serve hot.

Spinach Egg Thoran

 If you want a nutritious dish that does not comprimise on taste, try out this flavourful spinach or cheera egg thoran. The addition of egg cuts down the leafy bitterness and makes the dish more wholesome. My aunt Anitha often shares quick, easy and healthy recipes that I can try and this is one of my favourites.

Ingredients

- Spinach/*cheera* (2 bunch, leaves and stem chopped separately)
- Grated coconut (½ cup)
- Green chilli (½)
- Cumin seed powder (¼ tsp)
- Garlic (¼ tsp)
- Shallots (5, sliced)
- Curry leaves (1 sprig)
- Eggs (2)
- Turmeric powder (1 tsp)
- Pepper powder (½ tsp)
- Coconut oil as required
- Salt

Method

1. In a mixer, pulse the coconut, green chilli, cumin seed powder and garlic.

2. Heat oil in a pan and splutter mustard seeds. Add chopped shallots and curry leaves.

3. Add turmeric powder and pepper powder. Sauté lightly.

4. If you are using the spinach stem, add at this stage since it will take longer to cook than the leaves. Cover and cook till it wilts.

5. Add the ground coconut mix and sauté for a minute over low heat. Add salt as required.

6. Move the mixture to the sides of the pan, add 2 eggs and scramble. When the egg is half cooked, add the spinach leaves. Mix the egg and spinach, cover and cook for 2 minutes.

Note

- You can use the same recipe for drumstick leaves, red/green spinach or *palak*.

Pepper Chicken

I stayed in a college hostel, while studying in Bangalore. At that time, I spent most of the weekends at my aunt Julie's home. She would make me the yummiest home cooked meals. My favorite was her *pulissery, payar* and pepper chicken with plain rice. That along with her stories about the old times was a perfect combo. Here is a reproduction of her amazing and mouth watering pepper chicken recipe.

Ingredients

- Chicken (½ kg)
- Whole peppercorns (2 tbsp)
- Cashew nuts (5-6)
- Fennel seeds (½ tbsp)
- Water (1 cup)
- Ginger (1 big piece)
- Garlic (8 cloves)
- Onion (1 large, thinly sliced)
- Turmeric powder (1 tsp)
- Mustard seeds (1 tsp)
- Green chilli (2, slit)
- Curry leaves (2 sprigs)
- Coconut oil
- Salt to taste

Method

1. In a saucepan, boil the whole peppercorns and cashew nuts in 1 cup of water, with the lid closed for 5 minutes. Allow it to cool completely and then grind in the mixer into a fine paste, using a very little amount of water. If you add too much water while grinding, you may not get a very smooth paste.

2. Now add the fennel seeds and grind again really well into a creamy consistency and set aside.

3. Next, grind together garlic and ginger in a mixer and set aside.

4. To prepare the curry, heat a pan and add a generous amount of coconut oil. Splutter the mustard seeds and then add the ground ginger and garlic. Fry the ginger and garlic really well until the colour starts to change.

5. Add thinly sliced onion and curry leaves to it. Now, add the slit green chillies. Once the onions start to soften, add turmeric powder and sauté in the oil until its raw smell goes away.

6. Add the ground pepper and cashew paste to the masala and sauté well.

7. Now, add the chicken and some extra water, along with some salt to taste. Close it with a lid and cook on medium flame. Once the gravy starts to turn thick and the oil starts to separate from the gravy, turn off the heat.

8. This curry is very thick gravy and will go really with *appam, chapati, puttu* or *parotta*.

Fish Moilee

This mildly spiced fish curry is another one of my favorite dishes. This is a very lightly spiced coconut milk based stewed fish recipe. The fish is first gently fried and then simmered in coconut milk gravy along with black pepper and tomatoes. This is a tasty option that you can serve with *appam*, rice or bread.

Ingredients for Marination

- King fish (500 grams)
- Ginger paste (½ tsp)
- Garlic (½ tsp)
- Pepper (1 tsp)
- Lime juice (2 tsp)
- Turmeric powder (½ tsp)
- Salt (½ tsp)

Ingredients for the Gravy

- Onion (2)
- Ginger (3 inch piece, sliced thin and long)
- Garlic (10, sliced)
- Shallots (10, sliced)
- Green chilli (5, sliced)
- Curry leaves (4-5)
- Cinnamon stick (3 inch)

- Whole black pepper (10)
- Cloves (4)
- Cardamom (4)
- Carrot (1, cut into round slices)
- Tomato (1, sliced into round circles)
- Thin coconut extract (1½ cups)
- Thick coconut extract (1 cup)
- Oil (for frying and sautéing)

Method

1. Marinate the fish with ginger garlic paste, pepper powder, lime juice, turmeric powder and salt.

2. Shallow fry the fish pieces lightly for a minute on each side and keep aside. It should only be half cooked.

3. Heat oil in a wide bottomed pan. Add cinnamon stick, whole pepper, cloves, cardamom and sauté until fragrant.

4. Add onions, shallots, sliced ginger, garlic, green chilli and curry leaves.

5. When the onions turn pale brown, add the thin batch of coconut milk.

6. Add the sliced carrot and let it cook covered till the carrot is semi cooked. Now add the fish pieces.

7. Arrange the sliced tomato over the fish pieces and let it cook covered for 10 minutes.

8. Now add the first thick batch of coconut milk. Turn off the heat when it comes to a slight boil.

9. Serve hot with *appam* or bread.

Note

- If the coconut milk is too runny add 1 teaspoon of corn flour to the milk before adding to the fish.

Tomato Rasam

 Hot, tangy and peppery, this *rasam* is an absolute thriller! I absolutely love the *rasam* that is served along with the traditional Andhra meals. This recipe is made with *toor dal*, lots of pepper and tomatoes. You can have it as a soup or with rice. You need to adjust the level of spice as per your taste.

Ingredients for Dry Roasting

- Fenugreek seeds (½ tsp)
- Coriander seeds (1 tsp)
- Cumin seeds (1 tsp)
- Peppercorn (1½ tsp)
- *Toor dal* (2 tsp)
- Dried red chilli (3)
- Garlic cloves (2)
- Curry leaves (4)

Ingredients for Tempering

- Gingili oil (1 tablespoon)
- Mustard seeds (½ tsp)
- Ghee (1 tsp)
- Coriander leaves and stem (½ cup)
- Salt (1 tsp)

Other Ingredients

- Tamarind (gooseberry size)
- Water (1 cup)
- Ripe country tomatoes (3, medium size)
- Turmeric (½ tsp)
- Asafetida (1/8 tsp)

Method

1. On a low flame, dry roast all the *rasam* powder ingredients except turmeric and asafetida. There is no need to peel the garlic. Remove from heat and let it cool.

2. Add the turmeric powder and asafetida and grind it to a very fine powder. Set aside.

3. Soak the tamarind in 1 cup of water. Squeeze the tamarind to extract all the juices. Strain the liquid and set the tamarind juice aside.

4. In a saucepan, boil water and drop the tomatoes. Let it boil for 3 to 4 minutes.

5. Remove from heat and drain. Peel the skin and grind the tomatoes to a puree. Set aside.

6. Heat sesame oil in a pan and add in the mustard seeds and the curry leaves. Let it splutter.

7. Add the tamarind extract and the tomato puree. Add one cup water and let it come to a roaring boil.

8. Add the *rasam* powder and salt. Let it boil for two minutes. Switch off the flame and add the ghee and coriander leaves.

9. Serve hot with rice or have it as a soup.

Prawn Curry with Coconut

 This prawn curry with rice is home cooked comfort food. The prawn is cooked along with *kodampulli* (Malabar tamarind) and spices and then mixed with ground coconut. It is a simple, flavorful dish that goes best with Kerala *matta* rice. This is one of my all time personal favorites!

Ingredients

- Prawn (250 grams, medium sized, shelled and deveined)
- Shallot (10 + 4 for garnish, thinly sliced)
- Green chilli (2, sliced)
- Garlic (3 cloves, sliced)
- Chilli powder (1 tsp)
- Coriander powder (1 tsp)
- Turmeric powder (½ tsp)
- Fenugreek powder (¼ tsp)
- *Kodampulli* or Malabar tamarind (1)
- Coconut oil (1 tbsp)
- Grated coconut (¾ cup)
- Water (1 cup)
- Mustard seeds (½ tsp)
- Curry leaves (1 sprig)
- Salt

Method

1. In a kadai or chatti, mix shallots, green chilli, garlic, *kodampulli,* chilli powder, coriander powder, turmeric powder, fenugreek powder and salt with 1 tablespoon coconut oil. Mix it well.

2. To this add the prawns and keep aside for 15 minutes.

3. Add 1 cup water and cook covered for 8-10 minutes on a medium flame.

4. In the meanwhile, in a mixer, grind the coconut into a fine paste with 1 cup of water.

5. Once the prawn is cooked, add the coconut paste and mix well and let it boil for a minute, while stirring.

6. Transfer to a serving dish.

7. For garnish, heat 1 tablespoon oil in a small round bottomed pan and fry 4 sliced shallots.

8. Add ½ teaspoon Kashmiri chilli powder and curry leaves. Pour over the prawn curry. Serve warm with rice.

Mutton Stew

 Mutton stew brings back memories of Christmas holidays spent at my grandparents' house. As kids, we always spent Christmas holidays with grandparents and cousins. Christmas morning was spent ripping apart presents carefully packed by my mom and aunt. Those days our presents were usually plain old stationary. How thrilled were we to get pencils, sharpeners and note books! This is probably why I still love stationary to this day! The gift opening was followed by a fancy breakfast, usually featuring mutton stew and appams.

Ingredients

- Coconut oil or vegetable oil (3 tbsp)
- Mutton (marinated with salt and pepper, 500 grams)
- Whole pepper (1 tsp)
- Cinnamon (2 inch piece)
- Cardamom (4)
- Cloves (4)
- Finely sliced onion (2 large)
- Ginger (2 inch piece, sliced)
- Garlic (4, sliced)
- Cardamom powder (¼ tsp)
- Green chilli (2-3, slit)

- Garam masala powder (1 tsp)
- Fennel seeds (2 tsp)
- Pepper powder (1 tsp)
- Coriander powder (1 tsp)
- Potato (1 large, chopped)
- Thin coconut milk (1½ cups)
- Thick coconut milk (1 cup)
- Ghee (1 tbsp)
- Shallots (4-5)
- Cashew nuts (5)
- Curry leaves (1 sprig)

Method

1. Heat oil in the pressure cooker and lightly fry the whole spices – pepper, cardamom, cloves and cinnamon.

2. Add onions, green chilli, ginger, garlic and curry leaves. Sauté till the onions turn translucent (not brown).

3. Add garam masala, fennel seed powder, coriander powder and pepper powder. Lightly fry the spice powders.

4. Add the mutton pieces, mix well and pressure cook until the meat is soft.

5. In the meantime, boil cubed potatoes with salt and green chilli and set aside.

6. Now add the 2nd extract of coconut milk/thin milk. Add the boiled potato cubes, cardamom powder and cook for a few minutes.

7. Add the thick coconut extract and turn off the heat when it starts to bubble.

8. To prepare tempering, heat 1 tablespoon ghee. Fry the cashew nuts until golden brown. Remove and keep aside.

9. Into the same pan, add finely sliced shallots and curry leaves. Fry till the onions are nicely browned. Pour this tempering over the mutton stew and serve hot.

Pan Roasted Potatoes

This is a simple side dish that my colleague at work used to bring for lunch. The poor chap would hardly get a share in it, as it was mostly eaten by the rest of the team! Roasted potatoes are a huge favorite and goes with just about anything.

Ingredients

- Baby potatoes (3 cups)
- Turmeric powder (½ tsp)
- Oil
- Chilli powder (1 tsp)
- Garam masala (½ tsp)
- Salt as per taste

Method

1. Wash and cut the potatoes into halves. Keep the skin on.

2. Parboil the potatoes with half teaspoon salt in a saucepan, or microwave on high for 3 to 4 minutes. Drain the water.

3. Marinate the potatoes with salt and a teaspoon of oil.

4. Heat a heavy bottom pan or cast iron pan. Add 3 tablespoon of oil and let it get hot.

5. Add the potatoes to the pan. Let it sear on each side before tossing sides.

6. Once all the sides are roasted brown, turn off the heat and sprinkle chilli powder and garam masala powder.

7. If it is a cast iron pan, the heat from the pan will be sufficient. Otherwise on low flame, toss the potatoes so that it gets coated on all sides with the masala.

Chilli Chicken

 This is a popular Indo-Chinese dish. In India, this may include a variety of dry chicken preparations. My sister often makes this along with her famous bacon fried rice, which is the perfect combination. Chilli chicken is a safe bet whenever you are looking for a nice curry on the side.

Ingredients for the Batter

- Chicken (500 gram, cut into small pieces)
- Plain flour (3 tbsp)
- Corn flour (3 tbsp)
- Chilli powder (½ tsp)
- Pepper powder (½ tsp)
- Egg (2)
- Oil for frying

Ingredients for the Sauce

- Soya sauce (2 tbsp)
- Green chilli sauce (2½ tbsp)
- Tomato ketchup (2 tbsp)
- White vinegar (1 tsp)

Ingredients for the Gravy

- Oil (2 tbsp)
- Green chillies (3-4, slit)
- Garlic (1 tsp, finely chopped)
- Ginger (1 tsp, finely chopped)
- Onions (3, cut into 1 inch squares)
- Green capsicum (1, cut into 1 inch cubes)
- Spring onions (2-3, finely chopped)

Method

1. Separate the bony pieces of chicken to make the stock.

2. In a saucepan, boil the bony pieces with 3 cups of water, salt and a pinch of turmeric. Separate the chicken from the stock.

3. In a large bowl; mix together flour, corn flour, soya sauce, pepper powder, egg and add the chicken. Set aside for 15 minutes to an hour.

4. In a dish, shallow fry these chicken pieces, for a minute on each side, until half cooked. Keep the chicken pieces aside. You can also fry the chicken pieces that were used to make the stock.

5. In another wok or kadai, heat oil and add green chillies, chopped ginger and garlic.

6. Sauté for a minute or so and add the cubed onions. Stir fry on high heat for 2-3 minutes and add the capsicum.

7. In a small bowl, mix all the sauces together – green chilli sauce, soya sauce, tomato ketchup and vinegar. Add the sauces into the kadai.

8. Add the chicken pieces and mix well so that the sauce coats the chicken pieces.

9. Now add the chicken stock and let it cook for some time till it becomes thick gravy. Top with spring onions and serve with fried rice.

Baked Fish

 My sister, Tania shared this recipe a long time ago and it has been a favorite of mine ever since! The fish is first semi fried and then baked to perfection. This preparation goes very well with *pulao* rice and *appams*.

Ingredients

- Fish (400 grams, flat pieces with bone)
- Chilli powder for marination (2 tsp)
- Turmeric powder (1 tsp)
- Juice of 1 lime
- Vegetable oil (2 tbsp)
- Onion (2, chopped)
- Ginger garlic paste (2 tsp)
- Chilli powder (1½ tsp)
- Tomato (1, chopped)
- Vinegar (1 tbsp)
- Tomato sauce (2 tbsp)
- Salt

Method

1. Make a paste of chilli powder, turmeric powder and salt with a few drops of lemon juice. Marinate the fish with this paste.

2. Shallow fry the fish for a minute on each side and keep it aside.

3. In a pan, add 2 tablespoon oil and sauté onions, ginger and garlic till the onions turn translucent. Add chilli powder and fry till the raw flavor goes.

4. Now add the tomatoes, cover and cook till the tomatoes turn soft.

5. Now add tomato sauce and vinegar, mix and turn off the heat.

6. In a well greased baking dish, layer the base with a fourth of the tomato mix.

7. Now assemble the fish on top and then cover it with the rest of the tomato mix.

8. Bake at 180 degrees centigrade for 30 minutes and till the color turns brown.

Sambar

 My husband Rajiv studied in St. Joseph's Boys School, Bangalore. In those days, his school refectory served beef fry and steaming hot sambar with white rice. As soon as the class broke for lunch, the boys would run at full speed to the refectory. "Nothing can beat that historic sambar", he would say. Taking it on as a challenge, I attempted various versions of sambar. Finally, with this recipe I hit the nail on its head!

Ingredients to Pressure Cook

- *Toor dal* (¼ cup)
- Carrot (1, chopped)
- Brinjal (½ cup)
- Drum sticks (1, chopped into 3 inch pieces)
- Golden cucumber or *vellarika* (½ cup)
- Tomato (1, quartered)
- Green chilli (2)
- Shallots (5)
- Turmeric powder (a pinch)
- Water (as needed)

Ingredients to Dry Roast and Grind

- Fenugreek seeds (½ tsp)
- Coriander seeds (2 tsp)
- Dry red chilli (5-6)

Other Ingredients

- Tamarind (size of a small gooseberry)
- Sambar powder (½ tsp)
- Asafetida (¼ tsp)
- Jaggery (1 tsp)
- Coriander leaves (¼ cup)
- Mustard seeds (½ tsp)
- Cumin seeds (¼ tsp)
- Ghee (1 tbsp)
- Salt & water (as needed)

Method

1. Soak the tamarind in warm water for 10-15 minutes and take the extract. Set aside.

2. Pressure cook *dal* in water with turmeric powder for 1 whistle.

3. Chop the vegetables, tomato, golden cucumber, drumstick and carrot into large pieces. Open the cooker and add the vegetables, shallots, green chilli along with some salt and pressure cook again till all the vegetables are cooked. The *dal* will also be fully cooked by now.

4. In a *kadai*, dry roast fenugreek seeds, coriander seeds and dry red chilli till a nice aroma arises. Powder coarsely and add back into the *kadai*.

5. Now add sambar powder, asafetida & tamarind extract. Allow it to boil.

6. Add the boiled spice mix to the dal and mix well. Add jaggery & boil for some more time. Add coriander leaves.

7. Finally temper mustard seeds and cumin seeds in 1 tablespoon of ghee and pour over the sambar.

Pumpkin Errisherry

 This dish is also known as *"mathanga erriserry"* and it is one of my favorite vegetarian side dishes. It is an appetizing mix of roasted coconut and creamy cowpeas. This is a mild and tempered curry with light sweet tones and is a great choice for vegetarians. This along with plain rice is enough to make a meal very satisfying.

Ingredients

- Red cowpeas or *vanpayar* (1 cup)
- Pumpkin (4 cups, chopped into medium pieces)
- Turmeric powder (½ tsp)
- Water as required
- Salt to taste

Ingredients for Grinding

- Grated coconut (1 cup)
- Turmeric powder (½ pinch)
- Garlic cloves (4)
- Cumin (¼ tsp)
- Green chillies (2)

Ingredients for Seasoning

- Coconut oil (1-2 tbsp)
- Mustard seeds (½ tsp)
- Dry red chillies (4)
- Chilli powder (1 tsp)
- Curry leaves (a sprig)
- Grated coconut (1 cup)
- Shallots (5, finely chopped)

Method

1. Soak the red cowpeas in water overnight or for at least 4 hours.

2. Grind grated coconut, garlic cloves, turmeric powder, cumin and green chillies to a smooth paste and keep it aside.

3. To pressure cook the red beans, add water to cover the beans. Add turmeric powder, salt and cook for 2 whistles on medium heat. It should be half cooked and not mushy.

4. Add the cubed pumpkin pieces and continue to pressure cook for one more whistle. Mash the pumpkin pieces with a spatula. You can leave a few chunky pieces if you like.

5. Add the ground coconut paste and cook for 5-7 minutes on medium heat.

6. Heat coconut oil in a pan and splutter mustard seeds. Sauté shallots, dry red chillies, chilli powder and curry leaves.

7. Reduce heat and add half a cup of grated coconut and roast for a few minutes till brown. Be careful not to burn it.

8. Pour the seasoning over the curry and gently mix everything.

Chicken Ularthiyathu

 This is a good everyday chicken dish to have along with rice. I had this for the first time, when I went to my cousin Suli's house. The meal was sumptuous and I fell absolutely in love with this simple chicken preparation.

Ingredients to Cook Chicken

- Chicken (½ kg, boneless)
- Onion (½ sliced)
- Ginger (2" piece, crushed)
- Green chilli (2, slit)
- Black pepper powder (½ tsp crushed)
- Turmeric (½ tsp)
- Salt

Ingredients to Stir Fry

- Garlic (12, crushed)
- Onion (½ chopped)
- Dry red chilli (3)
- Garam masala (½ tbsp)
- Coriander (½ tbsp)
- Chilli powder (1 tbsp)
- Turmeric (1 tsp)
- Curry leaves (2 sprigs)
- Oil (4-5 tbsp)

Method

1. Into a heavy bottomed pot, add all the 'Ingredients to cook the chicken'. Mix, cover and cook on low heat till the chicken is cooked. There is no need to add extra water as water will get released from the chicken. Keep aside.

2. Heat a generous amount of oil in a kadai and splutter mustard seeds. Add dry red chilli and curry leaves. Fry onion and garlic until onions turn brown. Add turmeric powder, coriander powder, chilli powder and garam masala.

3. Once the masalas are well cooked, add the cooked chicken. Cover and cook over low heat for 5 minutes. Serve hot.

Paneer and Green Peas Masala

 This dish is a classic combination of paneer (Indian cottage cheese) with green peas. It is also popularly known as *"mattar paneer"* and originates from North India. It consists of peas and paneer in a tomato based sauce that is spiced with garam masala. It is often served with rice, *chapatis* and *rotis*.

Ingredients

- Paneer (200 gm, cubed)
- Onion (2, chopped)
- Garlic cloves (10-12, chopped)
- Ginger (2 inch, chopped)
- Bay leaf (1)
- Dry red chilli (1)
- Cardamom (1)
- Cumin seeds (1/3 tsp)
- Turmeric powder (1/3 tsp)
- Red chilli powder (1 tsp)
- Cumin powder (½ tsp)
- Coriander powder (½ tsp)
- Garam masala powder (1/3 tsp)

- Tomato puree (1/3 cup)
- Fresh green peas (1 cup)
- Dry fenugreek leaves (*kasuri methi*) or coriander leaves (½ tsp)
- Vegetable oil (4 tbsp)
- Salt to taste

Method

1. Roughly chop onions, ginger and garlic.

2. Heat the oil in a pan and sauté them all together until the onions turn translucent. Allow it to cool and grind to a paste.

3. Heat oil in a *kadai*, add dry red chilli, cardamom, bay leaf and cumin seeds. Fry for a few seconds.

4. Turn the heat to low and add turmeric powder, chilli powder, cumin powder, coriander powder and garam masala.

5. Add the ground paste and mix well. Let it cook until the oil separates from the masala.

6. Add tomato puree. Cover and cook for 5 minutes.

7. Add one cup of hot water and green peas. Cover and cook for 10 minutes on low flame.

8. Now add the cubed paneer. Keep the lid on and cook for another 5 minutes or until the oil appears on top.

9. Sprinkle *kasuri methi* or coriander leaves on top.

10. Mix well and serve hot with *naan* or *roti*.

Pulissery with Coconut

 Pulissery is a spiced butter milk side dish. It is made with golden cucumber and coconut, ground with spices. This is a traditional Kerala style dish and also known as *"moru curry"*. This seasoned yoghurt curry has a very subtle taste and goes very well with rice. It is a favorite of all my family members!

Ingredients for Grinding

- Grated coconut (¾ cup)
- Cumin seeds (1 pinch)
- Garlic (¼ tsp)

Ingredients for Cooking

- *Vellarikka* or golden cucumber (1 cup, cut into bite size pieces)
- Green chilli (2, slit)
- Turmeric powder (1 tsp)
- Garlic cloves (3, sliced)
- Ginger (¼" sliced)
- Cumin powder (1/8 tsp)
- Whisked yogurt (500 ml)

Ingredients for Tempering

- Fenugreek seed or powder (1/8 tsp)
- Mustard seeds (½ tsp)

- Shallots (4, sliced)
- Dry red chilli (2)
- Coconut oil (1 tbsp)
- Salt

Method

1. Peel the skin, remove the seeds and cut the cucumber into bite sized pieces.

2. Cook the golden cucumber, green chilli, garlic, ginger, cumin powder, turmeric powder and salt in half cup water until the cucumber pieces become tender and the water is almost dried up.

3. Grind grated coconut, cumin seeds and garlic with ¼ cup water to a smooth paste.

4. Over low heat, add the ground coconut mixture to the cooked cucumber and mix well till the raw flavor of coconut is gone.

5. Add the beaten yoghurt. Make sure that the heat is low, otherwise the curd will curdle. Once the mix gets warm, turn off the heat.

6. In another pan, heat oil and crackle the mustard and fenugreek seeds. Add dried red chilli, sliced shallots and curry leaves.

7. Fry till the onion turns golden brown. Add this to the *pullisherry* curry and mix well. Serve warm with rice.

Note

- You can also use ash gourd *(kumbalanga)* instead of cucumber *(vellarikka).*

Sun Dried Bitter Gourd Fry

 Bitter gourd does not usually sound very appetizing, but there are a variety of amazing dishes you can make out of this unique vegetable. This crispy fried sun dried bitter gourd dish can turn even a critic into an ardent fan of the vegetable.

Ingredients

- Bitter gourd (4, sliced)
- Turmeric powder (½ tsp)
- Green chilli (4-5, slit)
- Oil for frying
- Salt (1 tsp)

Method

1. Cut the bitter gourd into round slices.

2. Mix bitter gourd, salt, green chilli and turmeric powder with your hand and set aside for 15 minutes. Discard the water that will get released from the vegetable.

3. Place the bitter gourd in a kadai and cook on low heat. The remaining water will evaporate.

4. Toss the bitter gourd in the kadai to avoid it sticking to the bottom, but do not mix with a spoon as it can turn mushy.

5. Spread the bitter gourd on a baking sheet and sun-dry it for 3-4 days till it completely dries up.

6. Once it cools down, store it in an air tight container.

7. Heat oil in a pan. Once hot, turn down the heat to medium high. Add the dried bitter gourd and let it puff up. Remove onto a paper towel to drain off excess oil.

8. Serve it with rice or have it as a snack.

Note

- Cut the bitter gourd slightly thick. They shrink a lot once they get dried, so try making it in large quantity if you want to store it for future use.

- Make sure to sun-dry the bitter gourd completely and also cool it before storing for later use, or else they can get destroyed by fungus.

Sweets & Desserts

Carrot Cupcake & Cream Cheese Frosting

 This carrot cupcake is rich, moist and simply perfect when paired with cream cheese frosting. The added bonus is that this recipe uses wheat flour. The caramelized sugar is added to give it a rich brown color. This is a nice option when you want to treat someone to something special!

Ingredients for the Carrot Cupcake

- Wheat flour (1 cup)
- Baking powder (1 tsp)
- Baking soda (1 tsp)
- Cinnamon (1 tsp)
- Nutmeg (½ tsp)
- Salt (¼ tsp)
- Chopped walnuts (½ cup)
- Sugar (¾ cup)
- Egg (2)
- Oil (150 ml)
- Grated carrot (1½ cup)
- Dates (½ cup, pitted and chopped)
- Sugar for caramelization (3 tsp)
- Vanilla essence (1 tsp)

Ingredients for Cream Cheese Frosting

- Block cream cheese (225 grams, cold)
- Unsalted butter (½ cup/113grams, room temperature)
- Icing sugar (2½ cups, sifted)
- Vanilla extract (½ tsp)
- Salt (1/8 tsp)

Method for the Carrot Cupcake

1. Sift the flour, baking powder, baking soda, cinnamon and nutmeg. Add the chopped walnuts and keep aside.

2. To prepare the sugar syrup, melt the sugar with 1 teaspoon water in a small pan. The sugar will melt and turn into a golden amber color.

3. In a separate bowl, cream the sugar and eggs using an electric whisk.

4. Pour the oil in a thin stream while continuing to beat. Add vanilla essence.

5. Add the grated carrot, chopped dates and the sugar caramel syrup.

6. Now gently fold in the sifted flour and mix till everything is incorporated.

7. Pour into lined cupcake pans filling up to ¾ of each pan.

8. Bake in a preheated oven for 20 minutes at 180 degrees centigrade or till a toothpick inserted comes out clean.

Method for the Cream Cheese Frosting

1. Cream the butter, cream cheese and vanilla in a bowl until smooth and well combined.

2. Add sifted icing sugar little at a time while beating, till you get a smooth creamy texture. Add salt and vanilla extract. This will get you a soft pipe-able icing.

3. However if you need it to be stiffer, you can add additional icing sugar or 1 tbsp of corn flour if you don't want to increase the sweetness.

Note

- In warm climates, cream cheese frosting easily tends to get runny. To avoid this, take the cold cream cheese block out of the fridge just before you need to use it.

- Don't overbeat the cream cheese. It will get creamier and more difficult to pipe.

Pineapple Upside Down Cake

 This classic cake has been an all time favorite of my family! If you like pineapple, you will surely love this cake. It is a moist and buttery cake with caramelized pineapple on top. I'm sure that you won't be able to stop with just one slice of this delicacy.

Ingredients for the Cake

- Plain flour (1¼ cup)
- Baking powder (1 tsp)
- Baking soda (¼ tsp)
- Granulated sugar (1 cup)
- Vegetable oil (5 tbsp)
- Butter milk (¼ cup)
- Pineapple juice (¼ cup)
- Egg (1 at room temperature)
- Vanilla essence (1 tsp)
- Salt (¼ tsp)

Ingredients for the Topping

- Unsalted butter (5 tbsp, melted)
- Light brown sugar (½ cup)
- Round pineapple slices (7, fresh or tinned)

Method

1. Sift the flour, baking powder, baking soda and salt. Add the granulated sugar and mix well. Keep aside.

2. In another bowl, whisk the wet ingredients; egg, buttermilk, vanilla, pineapple juice and oil.

3. Mix the dry ingredients into wet ingredients in 3 parts.

4. Melt the butter and pour it into the cake pan. It should cover the base of the pan completely. Use the butter to grease the sides of the tin as well. Sprinkle brown sugar over the butter and arrange the pineapple slices on top of it.

5. Pour the batter into the pan and bake in a preheated oven at 180 degrees centigrade for 45 minutes or till a skewer inserted comes out clean.

6. Wait for it to cool down for 10 minutes and then gently flip the cake so that the pineapple comes on top.

7. Don't lift the pan till all the caramel juices come onto the cake. Leave it on for a few minutes and then lift the pan. Serve warm.

Coffee and Cinnamon Pannacotta

 Pannacotta is a rich and creamy dessert which originated in Italy. The sweetened cream thickened with gelatin is sometimes aromatized with coffee, vanilla or other flavorings. The perfect pannacotta should have a nice wobble when you shake it gently.

Ingredients for the Pannacotta

- Milk (½ cup)
- Instant coffee powder (2 tsp)
- Cinnamon stick (1)
- Fresh cream (2 cups)
- Sugar (½ cup)
- Vanilla essence (½ tsp)
- Gelatin (2¼ tsp)
- Warm water (3 tbsp)

Ingredients for the Caramel Praline

- Sugar (100 grams)
- Cashew nuts (¼ cup)

Method

1. Grease the inside of the ramekins or pudding cups with butter.

2. Heat milk along with cinnamon stick in a saucepan. Lower the heat once it starts boiling and add cream and sugar. Stir till the sugar dissolves.

3. Remove the cinnamon stick. Now add the coffee powder, vanilla extract and mix well.

4. Meanwhile, add the gelatin to cold water, dissolve and allow it to bloom for about 5-10 minutes.

5. Add this to the coffee-cream mixture and whisk until it is completely dissolved. Pour into the ramekins and refrigerate for 3-4 hours till it sets well.

6. To make caramel praline; take a small pan, heat sugar till it melts completely and turns into the color of honey.

7. Turn off the heat and add chopped cashew nuts. Immediately pour this in a thin layer onto a non-stick baking sheet or a well buttered clean surface. Once it completely cools down, break it into small pieces and coarsely grind the caramel praline with a mortar and pestle.

8. To serve, place the ramkeins in warm water so that it releases from the sides.

9. Flip it on to a serving plate and arrange the caramel praline around the pannacotta and serve chilled.

Banoffee Pie

As the name suggests, banoffee pie is a combination of banana, toffee and a pinch of coffee. This is a no bake dish with a buttery biscuit base. It has caramel toffee sauce and is topped with banana and cream. This is an excellent choice when you are looking for something sweet.

Ingredients for the Pie

- Digestive biscuits (150 grams)
- Melted butter (1/3 cup or 75 grams)
- Cinnamon powder (½ tsp, optional)

Ingredients for the Topping

- Caramel sauce (Recipe No: 97)
- Bananas (2, sliced)
- Heavy whipping cream (1 cup or 250 ml)
- Icing sugar (2 tbsp)
- Cocoa powder or chocolate flakes

Method

1. For the crust, crush the biscuits into a fine powder by using a food processor.

2. Stir the crumbs with melted butter and cinnamon until well moistened and press into the base of an 8 or 9 inch pie pan. Chill for at least 30 minutes until set.

3. Prepare the caramel sauce. Once it cools down, pour into the chilled crust. Chill in the fridge for a minimum of 1 hour or up to 24 hours.

4. With a hand mixer, whip the heavy cream with the icing sugar until soft peaks form.

5. To assemble, place the sliced banana on the toffee sauce and then top it generously with the whipped cream.

6. Garnish with chocolate flakes or cocoa powder and store in a fridge until ready to serve.

Christmas Plum Cake

 So many wonderful memories come to mind when I think of Christmas. For my family a lot of it revolves around baking and eating the traditional Christmas plum cake. After the early morning mass, we cousins would rush back home for the Christmas presents and the grand breakfast. It all begins with the grandparents cutting the cake, followed by homemade grape wine and then breakfast. My aunt Anitha, makes the best plum cakes that are perfectly moist and with just the right amount of fruits, nuts and spices. This is an adapted version of her cake recipe.

Ingredients for the Cake

- Butter (225 grams, softened)
- Eggs (4, separated)
- Powdered sugar (225 grams. Keep 4 tbsp of sugar separate)
- Flour (250 grams)
- Baking powder (1 tsp)
- Baking soda (½ tsp)
- Vanilla essence (1 tsp)
- Lime juice (1 tbsp)
- Cashew nuts (100 grams, lightly roasted, chopped)

Spice Powders

- Cinnamon (1 tsp)

- Nutmeg (¼ tsp)

- Cloves (½ tsp)

- Dry ginger powder (½ tsp)

Ingredients for the Caramelized Sugar Syrup

- Sugar (1 cup)

- Water (¼ cup)

Mixed Dry Fruits (275 grams)

Use any combination of dried fruits and citrus peels depending on what you prefer. You can also add dates, cranberries, dried pineapple, tutti-frutti, dry figs etc. Given below, is the combination of fruits that I use:

- Black raisins (140 grams)

- Yellow raisins (30 grams)

- Dry candied ginger (20 grams)

- Candied orange peel (50 grams)

- Glazed cherry (35 grams)

Method

1. Wash, dry and chop the raisins. Soak the mixed dry fruits in rum. Keep it in an airtight container for at least three days. Then drain the soaked dry fruits and retain the soaked rum for later use.

2. To prepare the caramel syrup; in a saucepan, combine 2 tablespoon water and one cup sugar. Cook until the sugar melts and turns golden brown in color. Switch off the flame and slowly add the rest of the water to the caramel. Turn the heat back on and stir well to combine. Set aside to cool.

3. Sift the flour, baking powder, baking soda, salt and spices.

4. Use 3 to 4 tablespoon of the same flour to toss and coat the cashew nuts and mixed fruits. This is so that they don't sink to the bottom of the cake.

5. Separate the egg yolk & white.

6. Using an electric beater, cream together butter, sugar and egg yolks until light and fluffy. Add vanilla essence, lime juice and the prepared caramelized sugar.

7. Gently fold in the flour. If the mix is too thick, you can add 1 or 2 tablespoon of milk.

8. Now gently fold in the flour coated fruits and nuts.

9. In the meanwhile, beat the egg whites to a stiff peak. Add 4 tablespoons sugar and beat again. Very gently, fold this into the cake batter.

10. Place the cake batter in a preheated oven and bake at 180 degrees centigrade for about 1 hour or until a toothpick inserted in the center comes out clean.

11. Remove the tin from the oven. When it cools down slightly remove from cake tin and set it on a wire rack to cool down.

12. Once the cake has cooled completely, sprinkle some more rum over it and cover it tightly with aluminum foil and store until ready to cut.

Dark Chocolate Caramel Tarts

 One of our favorite bakery items is the caramel tarts from Best Bakery in Cochin. It is a pastry tart filled with caramel toffee sauce, cashew nuts and raisins. In this recipe, I have also mentioned an optional topping of chocolate ganache over the toffee sauce. After all, a little bit of chocolate can't hurt right?

Ingredients for the Tart Shell

- Plain flour (1½ cups or 204 grams)
- Sugar (½ cup or 100 grams, powdered)
- Salt (½ tsp)
- Very cold butter (½ cup or 113 grams, cut into small cubes)
- Egg yolk (1 large, lightly beaten)
- Cold water (1-2 tsp)

Ingredient for the Topping

- Dark chocolate (100 grams, chopped into small bits)
- Cream (100 grams)
- A pinch of salt
- Caramel sauce (Recipe no: 97)

Method

1. For the pastry; in a bowl, combine flour, sugar and salt. Crumble in the butter cubes and mix till it becomes a coarse crumbly mix, resembling oat flakes.

2. Now add the egg yolk and bring the mixture together using a fork. If the mix is too dry add a tsp of cold water. Make sure you don't over work the dough with your hands; otherwise the heat from your fingers will melt the butter.

3. Form a flat disk shape with the dough, cover with a cling film and refrigerate for at least 30 minutes.

4. Place the dough between two sheets of cling film or parchment paper and roll to ¼ inch thickness. The cling film will ensure that the dough does not break.

5. Cut the dough into circles using a cookie cutter or any circular mould.

6. Grease the tart pan with butter. Place the dough in the pan and using your fingers, press the crust into the sides and bottom of the pan.

7. Use a knife to cut off the excess from the top of the tart pan. Poke holes on the base of the pastry using a fork.

8. Place the tart crust in the refrigerator of another 30 minutes or until you bake. It will keep the tart shell from puffing up too much in the oven.

9. In a preheated oven, bake the pastry shells for 12-14 minutes. The outer rim will turn golden brown first. Ensure that the inner part of the pastry is also done.

10. Let the baked tart shells cool for 10-15 minutes or a little longer before removing them from the molds.

11. Prepare the caramel sauce. Once it has completely cooled down, spoon it into the pastry tart shells.

12. To make the ganache; heat the cream in a saucepan. Turn off the heat when it starts to bubble and add the chopped chocolate. Mix well till you get smooth and shiny chocolate ganache.

13. Top the caramel sauce with an even layer of ganache.

14. Refrigerate till the ganache sets. Add a tiny sprinkle of salt on top.

Note

- The butter has to be very cold before adding to the tart pastry. Cut the butter into small cubes and then refrigerate before using.

- Instead of topping the tart with chocolate ganache, you can opt to add cashew nuts and raisins into the caramel sauce.

Easy Chocolate Cake

 This easy chocolate cake is a great recipe for a first time baker to try out. It is soft, kind of fudgy and oh so delicious! This also makes a great birthday cake and the kids will love it! Use double the quantity of ingredients to make a layer cake. I can assure you that no one will refuse a slice of this mesmerizing cake.

Ingredients for the Cake

- Plain flour (1 cup)
- Sugar (1 cup)
- Cocoa powder (½ cup)
- Baking powder (1 tsp)
- Baking soda (½ tsp)
- Butter milk (½ cup)
- Vegetable oil (¼ cup)
- Eggs (1, large)
- Vanilla extract (1 tsp)
- Freshly brewed hot coffee (½ cup)
- Salt (½ tsp)

Ingredients for Chocolate Ganache

- Semi sweet chocolate (200 grams)
- Heavy cream (180 grams or ¾ cup)
- Unsalted butter (20 grams)

Method

1. In a large bowl, whisk flour, sugar, cocoa, baking powder, baking soda and salt until well combined.

2. Add milk, vegetable oil, eggs and vanilla to the flour mixture. Using an electric whisk beat on medium speed until well combined.

3. Reduce speed and carefully add freshly brewed hot coffee to the cake batter until well combined. The batter will be thin, but don't worry about that.

4. Pour the batter into an 8 inch cake pan (greased with butter and lightly floured).

5. Bake in a preheated oven at 180 degrees centigrade for 40-45 minutes, until a toothpick inserted in the center of the chocolate cake comes out clean.

6. Remove from the oven and allow it to cool completely.

7. To make the ganache; in a saucepan, heat the cream until it starts bubbling. Pour this over the chopped chocolate and mix well till it is fully incorporated. Add butter and combine well.

8. Refrigerate until it becomes firm enough to spread.

9. To assemble, slice the cake into 2 layers using a serrated knife. Spread the ganache between each layer, over and around the cake. Store refrigerated.

Oreo Truffles

Oreo truffles are the perfect treat for any occasion! They are very easy to make and unbelievably appetizing. My seven year old nephew Jacob was taught to make this in his school. He recommended that I should definitely try it out. I did and I think you should too because you won't stop at one! Everyone loves these truffles!

Ingredients

- Vanilla flavored Oreos (30)
- Softened cream cheese (200 grams)
- Melted white chocolate (400 grams)

Method

1. Place the Oreos in a food processor or mixer and pulse until they form fine crumbs.

2. Alternatively, you can also crush the Oreos in a sealed plastic bag with a rolling pin.

3. Now add the cream cheese and pulse in bursts until well combined.

4. Scoop 1 tablespoon of the mixture at a time, form 1 inch balls and place on a tray.

5. Keep the tray in the freezer for 15 minutes.

6. Melt the white chocolate, by heating in a microwave for 1 minute.

7. Now take the Oreo truffles from the freezer and using a spoon dip in the white chocolate. Allow the excess to run off and place it back on the tray.

8. You can sprinkle with crushed Oreos or dark chocolate and allow the chocolate to set.

9. Store refrigerated, in an airtight container.

Lemon Sandwich Cookies

I love anything lemony as the taste is pleasant and the smell is refreshing! This is a basic sugar cookie recipe which is sandwiched with a lemon and white chocolate filling. They are easy to make and leave you with a burst of freshness!

Ingredients for the Sugar Cookies

- Unsalted butter (100 grams, softened)
- Caster sugar (100 grams)
- Egg (half of a large egg)
- Zest of 1 lemon
- Plain flour (210 grams, sifted)
- A pinch of salt

Ingredients for the Filling

- Cream (100 grams)
- White chocolate (300 grams, melted)
- Zest of a lemon

Method

1. Beat the butter, sugar and lemon zest for a minute, so that they combine.

2. Crack an egg into a bowl, lightly beat it. Measure out half of it and add it to the butter-sugar mix and beat it together.

3. Now add the flour and a pinch of salt and mix it together so that it all comes together.

4. Using your hands, form the dough into the shape of a ball.

5. On a lightly floured surface, roll out the dough into 4mm thickness.

6. Dip a cookie cutter in flour and cut out as many shapes as you can out of the dough. You can re-roll the excess again.

7. Transfer the cookies to a tray lined with baking paper.

8. Bake them in a preheated oven at 180 degrees centigrade for 7-9 minutes, until the edges are golden brown.

9. Move them to a cooling rack once they come out of the oven.

10. Melt the white chocolate for 30 seconds at a time in the microwave, till it is smooth and creamy.

11. Heat the cream in a saucepan. Add the lemon zest to this. Just when the bubbles start to appear, pour it into the white chocolate. Stir it all together.

12. Once it cools, refrigerate it for 30 minutes. Whip the mix gently so that it becomes light and fluffy.

13. Fill it into a piping bag and pipe it onto the centre of a cookie and sandwich it with the second cookie.

Caramel Custard

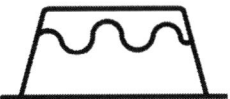 This is a no–nonsense creamy classic custard with a layer of clear caramel sauce. This easy dessert can be either be cooked in a steamer or baked in an oven. The smooth and creamy texture with the golden caramel syrup is a match made in heaven. For some reason, it always brings back memories of good ol' days.

Ingredients

- Sugar for caramelization (10 tbsp)
- Whole milk (500 ml or 2 cups)
- Sugar (½ cup)
- Eggs (4)
- Vanilla essence (1 tsp)
- Nutmeg powder (¼ tsp, optional)
- A pinch of salt

Method

1. To make the caramel; place 10 tablespoon sugar in an even layer in a saucepan.

2. Keep the flame on medium low. The sugar will melt and become brown in color. Ensure that the sugar melts evenly.

3. Switch off the heat once it reaches a golden brown color. You need to keep an eye on this, as the caramelized sugar can turn brown fast and taste bitter.

4. Pour this into a ramekin or pudding dish and swirl the dish so that it coats the base evenly. Now keep aside so that the caramel can harden.

5. To make the custard, add the eggs into a mixer and blend for a few seconds.

6. Then add the milk, sugar, vanilla essence, nutmeg powder and blend again for about 30 to 45 seconds.

7. Pour this into the pudding dish and cover it with an aluminum foil.

8. Boil water in a steamer.

9. Lower the heat and place the ramekins into the steamer and close the lid.

10. Simmer for 12 minutes and then switch off the fire and leave it for another 5 minutes.

11. Open the lid; allow it to cool down to room temperature. Refrigerate for 3 to 4 hours.

12. Very carefully flip the pudding onto another flat fish so that the caramel comes on top. Serve chilled.

No Bake Oatmeal Fudge Cookies

 These cookies made with peanut butter, oatmeal and cocoa powder are the quickest and tastiest no bake cookies that we can make at home. They are always good to have as a quick snack or with your afternoon tea or coffee. I usually make a bunch of them and store them for my family members who love these fudge cookies.

Ingredients

- Oats (240 grams or 3 cup)
- Butter (113 grams or ½ cup)
- Sugar (250 grams or 1¼ cup)
- Cocoa powder (25 grams or ¼ cup)
- Milk (120 ml or ½ cup)
- Crunchy peanut butter (160 grams or 2/3 cup)
- Vanilla extract (1 tsp)
- A pinch of salt

Method

1. In a sauce pan add butter, granulated sugar, milk, a pinch of salt and cocoa powder. Place it on the stove and cook over medium heat. Bring to a boil, stirring occasionally.

2. Once the mixture starts to boil, wait for exactly one and a half minute to get it to a rolling boil. Use a timer.

3. Now, remove the pan from the heat and stir in the oats, peanut butter and vanilla essence until fully combined.

4. Drop the cookie mixture onto the prepared baking sheets. Flatten it and allow it to cool down.

5. Then cover the tray with a plastic film and place the tray in the freezer for 20 minutes or until the cookies firm and set.

6. Store refrigerated in an airtight container.

Pineapple Layer Cake

 For this cake, you first prepare a normal sponge cake and then layer it with pineapple, whipped cream and praline. Since it has fresh pineapple, it is wonderfully moist and refreshing. This recipe makes a 6 inch layer cake. My husband loves this cake, probably since he has been a big fan of pineapple from his childhood days.

Ingredients

- Powdered sugar (½ cup + 1 tbsp /80 grams)
- Eggs, separated (2, at room temperature)
- Pineapple essence (¼ tsp)
- Water (½ tbsp)
- Plain flour (1/3 cup 45 grams)
- Corn flour (½ tbsp)
- Baking powder (¾ tsp)
- Whipping cream (¾ to 1 cup)
- Icing sugar (1-2 tbsp)
- Cubed pineapple (1 cup)
- Praline (½ cup)

Method for the Cake

1. Line a 6 inch round cake tin with parchment paper.

2. In a mixing bowl, combine together egg yolks, powdered sugar, pineapple essence and water. Beat for about 5 minutes or until it turns pale and thick. Keep aside.

3. In a clean and dry bowl, beat the egg whites until stiff peaks form. Keep aside.

4. Sift together plain flour, corn flour and baking powder 3 times.

5. Very gently fold in the flour mixture and egg whites alternately into the egg yolk mixture in 3 batches.

6. Immediately transfer the batter into the prepared cake pan and bake at 180 degrees centigrade for about 18 to 20 minutes or until a skewer inserted into the center of the cake comes out clean.

Method for the Layering

1. In a chilled bowl, beat whipping cream and icing sugar until soft peaks form. Keep aside.

2. Carefully cut the cake into two layers and place it on a plate.

3. Moisten the base sponge cake with pineapple syrup from the canned pineapple.

4. Cut the pineapple slices to small pieces. Keep aside.

5. Spread the whipped cream on the base layer and top with chopped pineapple.

6. Place the second layer on the base layer and drizzle the pineapple syrup on top. Spread the remaining whipped cream over the sides and top of the cake.

7. Decorate the sides of the cake with praline.

8. Garnish with pineapple pieces and praline. Refrigerate for 2 to 3 hours. Serve chilled.

Note

- To prepare praline, heat ¾ cup sugar in a heavy bottomed pan. When the sugar starts to caramelize; add half a cup of chopped cashew nuts and mix well until combined.

- Cook until the color changes to deep amber. Transfer the praline to a greased tray. Allow it to cool completely and crush it using a rolling pin.

Fudgy Chocolate Brownies

 What makes these brownies rich and fudgy is the high ratio of chocolate content. In comparison to a cake, a brownie is very easy to make. You don't need to beat air into it. It contains no rising ingredients and you don't have to worry about it rising. It is quite literally a cake walk, err.. I mean a brownie walk! Try out this recipe if you like your brownies extra fudgy with a crinkled top.

Ingredients

- Unsalted butter (100 grams)
- Dark chocolate (200 grams, chopped into small bits)
- Granulated sugar (1 cup or 225 grams)
- Brown sugar (¼ cup or 50 grams)
- Eggs (3, room temperature)
- Vanilla essence (1 tsp)
- Plain flour (¾ cup or 96 grams)
- Cocoa powder (¼ cup or 25 grams)
- Almonds or walnuts (½ cup, chopped)
- Salt (¼ tsp)

Method

1. Heat 150 grams chocolate in the microwave for 30 – 60 seconds until it has completed melted. In a separate bowl, melt butter. Mix the chocolate and butter until both are well incorporated. Keep aside 50 grams of chopped chocolate to add into the batter later.

2. Sift the flour and cocoa powder and keep aside.

3. In a bowl, add granulated sugar and brown sugar. Now add the eggs and add vanilla essence.

4. Using an electric whisk or hand whisk, beat this until all the sugar has melted.

5. Into this, pour the melted butter and chocolate and continue to whisk until well incorporated.

6. Fold in the sifted flour and cocoa powder.

7. Now add the remaining chopped chocolate and nuts.

8. Pour this into a lined baking tray.

9. Bake in a preheated oven at 170 degree centigrade for 20-25 minutes. Unlike a cake, a toothpick inserted into a brownie should come out with moist crumbs.

10. The top of the brownie may have slight cracks. You may need to adjust the timing and temperature according to the oven that you use.

11. Allow the brownie to cool completely in the pan before cutting. This can take about 3 to 4 hours.

12. Cut into squares and serve.

Note

- The brownie will continue to cook and harden after you take it out of the oven.

- To ensure a clean cut, use a large knife, wait for the brownie to cool completely and wipe the knife clean between cuts.

Jam Roll

 This is a thin sponge cake with a layer of jam, which is then rolled up like a log. Instead of jam, you can also fill it with cream and you will have what is known as a Swiss roll! This is a recipe that my mother used to make frequently when we were kids. This is a delectable sweet preparation that is a treat to the eyes too!

Ingredients

- Plain flour (85 grams)
- Corn flour (1 tbsp)
- Baking powder (1½ tsp)
- Eggs (4)
- Caster sugar (160 grams + 2 tbsp)
- Vanilla essence (1½ tsp)
- Water (1 tbsp)
- Strawberry jam (1½ cups)

Method

1. Line a 12"x 8" baking tray with parchment paper.

2. Sift the flour, baking powder and corn flour.

3. Separate the eggs and beat the egg yolks with caster sugar, vanilla essence and water until it is thick.

4. In a clean and dry bowl, beat egg whites until stiff.

5. Fold the egg yolk and egg white mix alternately into the flour mixture, very carefully, without allowing the bubbles to subside.

6. Pour the batter into the cake tin and bake immediately in a pre heated oven at 180 degrees centigrade for about 8 to 10 minutes or until golden brown on top. A toothpick inserted into the center of the cake should come out clean.

7. Allow the cake to cool for 2 minutes. Spread a baking sheet on the counter top and dust with powdered sugar.

8. Carefully flip the cake over the powdered sugar and gently peel off the baking paper.

9. Spread the jam evenly on top.

10. Carefully roll the cake tightly to form a cylinder while still warm. Make sure that you finish rolling the cake before the cake cools completely.

11. Wrap the jam roll with the same parchment paper and refrigerate for at least 1 hour.

Sugiyan

I had no idea that something like this existed, until my house help Sarasamma one day, whipped up this delicious fried thing. I was amazed to know that our humble green gram could be turned into something so scrumptious and delicious. This can be considered as a Malayali version of a doughnut, only tastier and healthier. These ping pong ball sized fritters are eaten as an evening snack along with *chaaya* (tea).

Ingredients for the Filling

- Green gram or *cherupayar* (1 cup)
- Jaggery (1½ cup, crushed)
- Grated coconut (½ cup)
- Cardamom powder (½ tsp)
- Cumin seed powder (¼ tsp)

Ingredients for the Batter

- Plain flour (½ cup)
- Rice flour (2-3 tbsp)
- Turmeric powder (1 pinch)
- Water (as required)
- Coconut oil (for deep frying)
- Salt (¼ tsp)

Method

1. Soak the green gram in water for 3 hours. Pressure cook the green gram with 1½ cup water, drain well and set aside. Make sure that the green gram is not overcooked.

2. Melt jaggery in little water and strain to remove any impurities.

3. Again boil the strained jaggery and add the grated coconut; mix well and continue stirring.

4. When the mixture starts thickening, add cooked green gram, cardamom powder and mix well. Continue stirring, till the mixture thickens completely.

5. Remove from heat and allow it to cool. Then make medium sized balls out of the mixture.

6. To make the batter, in a bowl, add plain flour, rice flour, turmeric powder, salt, enough water and make a smooth and thick batter without any lumps and set aside.

7. Heat coconut oil in a pan for deep frying. When it is hot, reduce heat to low.

8. Dip each ball in the prepared batter and deep fry them in oil, till the sugiyan turns golden in color.

9. Remove from oil and transfer to a kitchen paper towel. Serve hot.

Lemon Drizzle Cake

 If you are addicted to lemon flavors, this cake is just what the doctored ordered! This is a moist buttery lemon cake with a refreshing lemon drizzle over it. This is a very good option to consider during your 4:00 PM tea time with family.

Ingredients for the Cake

- Unsalted butter softened (175 grams)
- Caster sugar (175 grams)
- Eggs (3)
- Plain flour (175 grams)
- Baking powder (1 tsp)
- Salt (½ tsp)
- Zest of 2 lemons

Ingredients for the Drizzle

- Juice of 1 lime
- Caster sugar (4 tbsp)
- Water (4 tbsp)

Method

1. In a bowl, beat butter and caster sugar until pale and creamy. Then add the eggs, one at a time, slowly mixing through.

2. Sift in flour and baking powder. Add the lemon zest and mix until well combined.

3. Line a 7 inch baking pan and then spoon in the mixture and level the top.

4. Bake in a preheated oven at 180 degrees centigrade for 40-45 minutes until a skewer inserted into the centre of the cake comes out clean.

5. For making the lemon drizzle, boil water, sugar and juice of 1 lime till you get a syrupy consistency.

6. Prick the warm cake all over with a skewer or fork and then pour the drizzle over the cake.

7. Leave in the tin until completely cool, then remove and serve.

Marble Cake

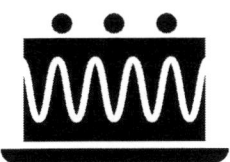 Marble cake is one of the most frequently prepared tea cakes at home. This particular recipe is a butter cake with vanilla and chocolate swirled very lightly by blending the light and dark batter to create a marbled effect. This cake is surely a treat for your eyes and your taste buds!

Ingredients

- Butter (200 grams, softened)
- Powdered sugar (200 grams)
- Eggs (4, approx 200 grams)
- Flour (190 grams)
- Baking powder (1 tsp)
- Vanilla extract (1 tsp)
- Cocoa powder (1½ tbsp)
- Milk (3 tbsp)

Method

1. Sift the baking powder and flour together thrice.

2. Beat butter and caster sugar together. Then add 4 eggs, one at a time, mixing well after each addition.

3. Fold in the flour, 2 tablespoon milk and 1 teaspoon vanilla extract until the mixture is smooth.

4. Keep aside ¼th of the batter. Dilute the cocoa powder in 1 tablespoon milk and stir this cocoa powder mix into the ¼th portion of the batter.

5. Prepare a 9 inch cake tin with parchment paper.

6. Using 2 spoons, dollop the chocolate and vanilla cake mixes into the tin alternately.

7. When all the mixture has been used up, take a fork and create swirls in the batter to create a marbled effect. Don't overdo it.

8. Tap the bottom on your work surface to ensure that there aren't any air bubbles.

9. Bake the cake in a preheated oven at 180 degrees centigrade for 45-55 minutes until a skewer inserted into the centre comes out clean.

Pineapple Sago Payasam

 This simple payasam was commonly made by the older generations since many decades. It is made with pineapple, sago and milk as the main ingredients. The first time I had it was when I visited my aunt Anita and I have loved it ever since.

Ingredients

- Sago (1 cup)
- Water
- Condensed milk (¾ tin)
- Whole milk (1 liter)
- Pineapple (diced, 2 cups)
- Cardamom (2, remove the peel and grind the seeds)
- Sugar (2 tbsp)

Method

1. Cut the pineapple into half inch small pieces and cook covered with 2 tablespoon sugar over a low flame till the pineapple is cooked through. Turn off the flame and let it cool completely.

2. In the meanwhile; cook the sago in 4-5 cups of water until it becomes translucent. It will soak up a lot of water and increase in volume.

3. In a large saucepan, boil milk and condensed milk, while stirring.

4. Add the cooked sago and ground cardamom and let it continue to cook for a few more minutes. Add more sugar, if you like it sweeter.

5. Turn off the heat and let it come to room temperature. It will get thicker as it rests. Stir in the caramelized pineapple.

6. Additionally, you can add nuts and golden raisins fried in a tablespoon of ghee. Refrigerate and serve chilled.

Fruit Parfait

 Parfait is basically a combination of fruits, yoghurt, granola and a bit of honey for sweetness. It can be had for a quick breakfast, a mid day snack or even as an after meal dessert. You must serve it in clear glass or mason jars so that the layering is visible. Based on what you have in your kitchen, feel free to play around with the combination of fruits, toppings, nuts, seeds, syrups and sauces.

Ingredients

- Mixed fruits
- Vanilla yoghurt
- Granola
- Honey

Method

1. Add a layer of granola in a parfait glass.
2. On top of the granola add a layer of vanilla yoghurt.
3. Top it with sliced mixed fruits and a drizzle of honey.
4. Repeat the layering, garnish and serve chilled.

Note

You can use a variety of fruit combinations such as:

- Nutty banana parfait: Banana with swirls of peanut butter, granola and yoghurt

- Vanilla cookie parfait: Vanilla yogurt, strawberry, chocolate chips and crumbled Oreos.

- Mixed fruits parfait: Mango, pineapple, banana, dates, melons, vanilla yogurt, granola and honey.

- Apple cinnamon parfait: Apple, golden raisins, cinnamon powder, vanilla yogurt and granola.

No Fail Vanilla Cupcake

 This recipe is a must have in your food diary. My 11 year old niece Sasha tried this on her own and it turned out perfect! This is a basic vanilla cupcake recipe and you can play around with the topping or frosting depending on what you like.

Ingredients

- Plain flour (125 grams)
- Baking powder (1 tsp)
- Caster sugar (125 gram)
- Baking soda (¼ tsp)
- Unsalted butter (125 gram)
- Large eggs (2)
- Milk (1½ tbsp)
- Vanilla extract (½ tsp)
- Salt (¼ tsp)

Method

1. Into a large bowl, sift together flour, baking powder, salt, caster sugar and baking soda.

2. Add 2 large eggs and soft unsalted butter.

3. Beat everything together for 1 minute on medium speed.

4. Add 1½ tablespoon of milk and vanilla extract. Beat again for another 30 seconds.

5. Scoop into lined cupcake pans till ¾ of each mould is filled.

6. Bake in a preheated oven at 170 degrees centigrade for 20-25 minutes.

Note

- Use softened butter. It should be soft enough that your finger will make an imprint with zero resistance, but not so soft that the butter looks shiny or greasy. Butter that is too soft won't aerate properly when beaten and will end up making your cake dense.

Unnakaya

The first time I had this spindle shaped sweet dessert was at a Kerala food festival in Bangalore. It tasted so unique, rich and yet so simple that I simply had to go back home and try it. It is a very popular snack in the Malabar region. Don't you just love the variety of dishes from the Malabar cuisine?

Ingredients

- Plantain (2, medium ripe)
- Oil for deep frying
- Cashew nut (2 tbsp, chopped)
- Raisins (2 tbsp, chopped)
- *Aval* or flattened rice (4 tbsp)
- Grated coconut (1 cup)
- Sugar (2 tbsp)
- Cardamom powder (2 pieces)
- Ghee (2 to 3 tsp)

Method

1. To prepare the filling, heat the ghee in a pan and fry cashew nuts and raisins until it turns golden.

2. Now add grated coconut and sauté till it turns golden. Add sugar and mix.

3. Add flattened rice, mix well and remove from fire.

4. Add cardamom powder, mix well and allow it to cool.

5. Steam the plantain until it gets soft. Allow this to cool slightly. Mash it well, till it becomes like dough.

6. Grease your hands with ghee and take a lemon sized portion of the prepared plantain and lightly flatten it using your finger tips.

7. Place 2 teaspoon of the prepared coconut filling in the center and press the edges together and roll it to form a cylindrical shape with pointed edges.

8. Heat oil in a pan and deep fry the stuffed plantain until golden brown on all the sides.

Note

- Do not use over ripe plantains.

- If you are finding it difficult to shape cooked plantain, add a teaspoon of rice flour to it and knead well until firm.

No Bake Mango Cheese Cake

 This is a great recipe to try out during the summer when mangos are in season. My cousin Suli, loves experimenting with sweets and desserts. The best part is that whenever she comes home, she brings her dishes along! This is one of her no fail, easy puddings that you can easily whip up in one bowl.

Ingredients

- Marie biscuit (1 pack)

- Butter (100 grams)

- Yoghurt (100 grams)

- Fresh cream (100 grams)

- Condensed milk (1 tin)

- Gelatin (1 heaped tbsp, dissolved in 3 tbsp cold water)

- Mango (1, ripe)

Method

1. Melt the butter in the microwave.

2. Powder the biscuit using a rolling in, until fully crushed, or blitz it in the food processor.

3. Mix the melted butter and powdered biscuit and press it on to the base of the pudding dish.

4. Meanwhile, add the gelatin to cold water, dissolve and allow it to bloom for about 5-10 minutes.

5. In a mixer, add mango and blitz it to form a puree. Now add yoghurt, fresh cream, condensed milk and gelatin and beat everything together until it forms a smooth mixture.

6. Pour the mix over the biscuit base. Allow it to set in the refrigerator for 4-5 hours.

7. Serve chilled.

Unniappam

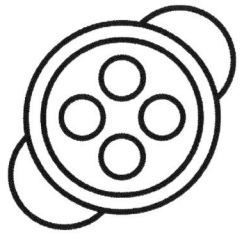 On my husband's behest, my mom makes these gorgeous unniappams, whenever she comes to visit us in Bangalore. The main differentiator in this recipe is that, it is made using wheat flour. This is easy to prepare and turns out soft every single time. The only thing that you need to make this work is a good unniappam chatti. We use an heirloom brass chatti and it does the job superbly.

Ingredients

- Wheat flour (1½ cups or 200 grams)
- Rice flour (½ cup, coarse)
- Jaggery (250-300 grams)
- Water (1 cup)
- Banana (½ a banana, *poovan pazham*, ripe)
- Coconut bits (½ cup)
- Ghee (1 tbsp)
- Black sesame seeds (1 tbsp)

Method

1. Heat ghee in a pan and add the coconut pieces. Fry until it turns golden brown.

2. Melt the jaggery in 1 cup of water, strain and keep aside.

3. Grind the banana in the mixer, add 2 tablespoon of the melted jaggery and grind again till you get a smooth paste.

4. Combine wheat flour, rice flour, the banana puree and the remaining warm melted jaggery. Pour more water, to get a consistency which is slightly thicker than that of *idli* batter.

5. Add fried coconut pieces and sesame seeds. Mix well and keep aside for 4-5 hours for fermentation.

6. Heat oil in an *unniappam chatti*. When the oil is hot, reduce the flame to medium and pour a tablespoon of batter into each hole.

7. After 2 to 3 minutes, turn the unniappams using a fork. Cook until it turns golden brown. Drain on a kitchen paper towel.

Note

- You can add 2-3 powdered cardamoms and 1/8 teaspoon ginger powder if desired.

- Adjust the quantity of jaggery according to your taste.

Banana Oat Muffins

This is a great recipe to try out when you have too many over ripe bananas at home. These muffins are fluffy, healthy and totally yummy! The recipe calls for basic ingredients and you can mix them all together in one bowl. Too good to be true? Nope. Try out this recipe today!

Ingredients

- Oats (2 cups or 200g)
- Baking powder (1 tsp)
- Baking soda (½ tsp)
- Cinnamon powder (½ tsp)
- Ripe banana (3, *robusta* variety)
- Oil (½ cup or 125 ml)
- Sugar (½ cup, brown or white)
- Vanilla extract (1 tsp)
- Eggs (2)
- Mix of raisins/chocolate chips/walnuts (1 cup)
- Salt (¼ tsp)

Method

1. In a mixer, grind the oats to make fine flour.

2. Into a bowl, add the oat flour, baking powder, baking soda, salt and cinnamon powder. Mix everything together so that it gets evenly distributed and keep it aside.

3. In another bowl, mash the ripened bananas. Now add the rest of the ingredients – sugar, eggs, oil, raisins, walnuts and vanilla extract. Mix them all together to form a uniform mixture.

4. Add the flour mix into the wet mix and combine them all together to form the muffin batter.

5. Prepare the muffin tin with cupcake liners. Transfer the batter onto the muffin tray, filling 2/3 of each cup.

6. Bake the muffins in a preheated oven at 180 degrees centigrade for 20-24 minutes.

Parippu Payasam

 Onam is one of the most loved festivals in Kerala and the highlight of the Onam season is usually *payasam*. Kerala has an amazing array of wonderful *payasams* and this is one of the most popular of them. This recipe can serve around 20 people.

Ingredients

- Split moong dal or *cherupayar parippu* (2½ cup or ½ kg)
- Cooked sago (1 cup, optional)
- Jaggery (1 kg)
- Whole coconut (1½, grated, to extract milk)
- Cardamom (10)
- Dry ginger powder or *chukku podi* (¼ tsp)
- Cumin powder (¼ tsp)
- Coconut pieces cut into very small bits (½ cup)
- Cashew nuts (½ cup)
- Raisins (½ cup)
- Ghee (4 tbsp)
- First extract of the coconut milk (thick extract, 1½ cup)
- Second extract of coconut milk (thin extract, 3-4 cups)

Method

1. In a heavy bottomed pan or *urali*, dry roast the *dal* until the color changes to golden and becomes fragrant. Once it cools down, wash it in water and set aside to drain.

2. In a large pressure cooker, add 4 cups of water. Pressure cook the *dal* in it. It should be well very well cooked.

3. Mash the *moong dal* with the back of a spatula. To make it quicker, you can use a hand blender to ensure that there are no lumps.

4. Meanwhile, melt the jaggery in water. The jaggery syrup should not be too thick.

5. Add cooked sago to the *moong dal*.

6. Strain the jaggery syrup into the dal. Let it boil. The dal should cook further in the jaggery syrup until the quantity reduces to half. Keep stirring.

7. Add the thin coconut milk, mix well and allow it to come to a boil again. Stir continuously over medium heat until the mixture thickens.

8. Finally add the thick coconut milk and cook for a minute on low heat and switch off the flame. Keep stirring until the milk is incorporated. Do not boil the coconut milk.

9. Turn off the heat and add cumin powder, dry ginger powder and cardamom powder. Mix well.

10. Heat 2 tablespoon ghee in a heavy bottom pan. Fry the coconut pieces until brown. Remove and set aside.

11. Fry the cashew and raisins and set all these aside. Finally add the fried cashews, fried raisins, coconut bits and 1 tablespoon ghee.

12. Serve warm or cold. Enjoy!

Note

- The sago is added to give the payasam texture. To cook sago, boil it in water till it swells up and becomes translucent. Drain off the excess water.

- Make sure that the dal is cooked well before adding the jaggery.

Carrot Halwa

 This dessert is also popularly known as *"gajar ka halwa"* and is very common in north India. It is made by cooking grated carrot with water, milk, sugar, and cardamom. Warm carrot halwa with vanilla ice cream is a great choice for a hot and cold dessert. You usually get this dessert at most wedding ceremonies in India.

Ingredients

- Carrot (500 grams, approx 4 cups)
- Milk (2 cups)
- Sugar (1 cup)
- Ghee (1 to 2 tbsp)
- Cardamom powder (2, crushed)
- Cashew nuts or pistachios (5)

Method

1. Wash the carrot and peel them. Grate the carrot to medium thickness.

2. In a saucepan, add the milk and grated carrots.

3. Turn on the heat and cook on low-medium flame until all the milk is absorbed.

4. Keep stirring continuously. Once the milk has evaporated, add sugar and cook for another 15-20 minutes.

5. The sugar will melt and turn gooey. Keep stirring. When the moisture has half evaporated, add 1 tablespoon ghee. Add cardamom powder and stir well.

6. In a small pan, heat 1 tablespoon ghee, fry cashew nuts and raisins.

7. Pour this over the carrot halwa. Garnish with chopped nuts and serve warm.

Note

- You can also add 2 tablespoon of condensed milk along with the sugar for added flavor.

White Pudding with Chocolate Sauce

 This is a very easy pudding to make as a quick dessert. You can use this as a base recipe to add more items like caramelized pineapple, crumbled Oreos, other add-ins or eat it plain. It is creamy and delicious and definitely gives you the much needed sugar rush.

Ingredients

- Condensed milk (1 tin)
- Milk (2 tins)
- China grass (10 grams)
- Water (¾ cup)

Ingredients for the Chocolate Sauce

- Eggs (2)
- Milk (2 cups)
- Sugar (¾ cup)
- Cocoa powder (1 tbsp)

Method

1. Soak the China grass in 1 cup water for 30 minutes.

2. In a saucepan, boil milk and condensed milk over medium heat, while stirring.

3. Now melt the China grass by boiling the water, and add to the milk mixture through a strainer.

4. Remove from fire and pour into a pudding dish. Once it cools down, cover and keep in the fridge to set for 3 to 4 hours.

5. To make the chocolate sauce; beat 2 eggs well. To this, add the milk and sugar.

6. Double boil this to a thick consistency. Mix cocoa powder in 1½ tablespoon of hot water and add to the milk mixture by straining. Mix well.

7. Once the white pudding has set, pour the chocolate sauce over it and serve chilled.

Accompaniments

Mayonnaise

Who doesn't love a good mayonnaise? This sauce or dressing can be used in burgers, sandwiches, salads or even as dips. There are multiple ways to prepare mayo, but it cannot get simpler than using the using the stick blender method. All it takes is a mere 30 seconds! You should try it out today if you don't believe me!

Ingredients

- Egg (2, at room temperature)
- Any unflavored oil (200 ml)
- Garlic (½ tsp)
- Mustard sauce (¼ tsp)
- Sugar (½ tsp)
- Salt (¼ tsp)
- Vinegar or lime juice (½ tsp)

Method

1. Put all the ingredients into the narrow bowl of the stick blender.
2. Hold the whisk to the floor of the bowl and turn it on.
3. In 30 seconds, you will see it begin to foam around the whisk.
4. Now gently whisk it in up and down motion till the whole mix is turned into a thick mayonnaise.
5. Pour it into a bowl and refrigerate to increase thickness.

Chukku Kaapi

 This spiced coffee drink is absolutely brilliant when you have a cold, sore throat or a fever. The aroma of the pepper and spices while brewing this drink in itself will awaken your senses. On a cold day when you feel low, this drink works like magic!

Ingredients

- Water (3 cups)
- Ground pepper (½ tbsp)
- Dry ginger (1 inch piece, coarsely ground with mortar and pestle)
- Cumin seeds (½ tbsp)
- Cardamom (2)
- Nutmeg (¼)
- Mexican mint or *panikoorka* (2 leaves)
- *Tulasi* leaf or holy basil (2 or 3)
- Coriander seeds (½ tbsp)
- Jaggery (2 tbsp)
- Instant coffee powder (1 tsp)

Method

1. In a saucepan, boil all the ingredients, except the coffee powder.
2. Keep the pan covered.
3. Turn off the heat and add the coffee powder.
4. Strain and drink while hot.

Mint Ginger Lime Concentrate

 The beauty of a concentrate is that you can keep it around for ages. Whenever the mood strikes, you can dilute the concentrate with water and ice. Isn't it good to have a refreshing cold drink ready for you at all times? This drink is best to consume on a hot summer day when you are sweating and need that extra dose of water in your body!

Ingredients

- Ginger (100 grams)
- Lime (15 or 1½ cup juice)
- Sugar (1 kg)
- Water (2 glasses)
- Mint leaves (1 cup)
- Green food color (optional)

Method

1. Slice ginger and grind in the mixer with half cup water. Strain the juice and set this aside for two hours. White sediment will settle at the bottom.

2. Juice the lime and filter to remove the seeds.

3. In a vessel, add the sugar and water and let it boil. Once the sugar has melted, add the mint and continue to let it boil till it reaches single stand consistency.

4. Then turn off the heat and let it cool.

5. The next day, strain the mint and sugar concentrate.

6. Add the ginger juice without disturbing the white sediment.

7. Now add the filtered lime juice and stir with a ladle. Add mint green food color if you like.

8. Pour into bottles and keep refrigerated.

9. To prepare juice, pour 3-4 tbsp of the concentrate into a glass and add one can of soda or cold water. Stir and serve cold.

Hung Yoghurt Dip

 One of the cons of working from home during the lockdown is the frequent urge to munch on snacks. Carrots and cucumbers strips with this hung yoghurt dip turned out to be the perfect pandemic lockdown snack. The best part is that the dip is healthy and lip-smacking at the same time!

Ingredients

- Yogurt or thick curd (1 cup)
- Garlic (2 cloves, minced)
- Black olives (2 tsp, chopped)
- Mustard sauce (1 tsp)
- Spring onions (1 tbsp, finely chopped)
- Chilli flakes
- Extra virgin olive oil
- Salt to taste

Method

1. Spoon yogurt into a cheese cloth and place the sieve on top of a vessel for an hour in the refrigerator. All the whey will drip down in the vessel, leaving thick curds.

2. Whisk in the garlic, spring onions, chopped olives, mustard sauce, salt and mix.

3. Sprinkle with chilli flakes and drizzle with olive oil just before serving.

4. Serve an assortment of carrots, cucumbers, breads and chips alongside the dip.

Beef Pickle

For my foodie husband Rajiv, beef pickle is something that he can have anywhere and anytime! For him a good pickle with rice and some *manja moru* (Kerala style seasoned buttermilk) is more than enough to complete the meal. When that is pickle made of beef, well, there's nothing to complain about!

Ingredients for Marination

- Beef (300 grams, cleaned and cut into 1cm cubes)
- Turmeric powder (½ tsp)
- Chilli powder (1 tsp)
- Garam masala (1 tsp)
- Pepper powder (1 tsp)
- Vinegar (1 tbsp)
- Salt (½ tsp)

Ingredients for Frying

- Vegetable oil (for frying)
- Gingili oil (1 cup)
- Vinegar (100 ml)
- Ginger (¼ cup, cut into thin slices)
- Garlic (½ cup, sliced)
- Ginger garlic paste (4 tbsp, pulsed in blender to a coarse paste)
- Chilli powder (3 tbsp)
- Garam masala (1 tsp)
- Turmeric powder (½ tsp)
- Asafetida (½ tsp)
- Fenugreek (¼ tsp)
- Mustard powder (1 tsp)
- Salt to taste

Method

1. Cut the beef into small pieces. Marinate and set aside for 20 minutes.

2. Pressure cook the beef cubes with enough water for one whistle. Drain the remaining water and keep it aside.

3. Heat vegetable oil in a large kadai. Add the beef pieces, wait for the bubbles to subside and fry the beef until it turns dark brown in colour. Remove and set aside.

4. Now in a separate pan, heat gingili oil.

5. Add sliced ginger and garlic and sauté well. Remove the ginger and garlic from the oil.

6. Now add the ginger and garlic paste. Sauté till the raw flavor goes and everything is fried well, but do not make it brown. Remove this from the oil.

7. Switch off the fire. Wait for a minute and add chilli powder, turmeric powder, garam masala, fenugreek powder, mustard powder and asafetida. Stir well. This way the powders will not get burnt.

8. Now turn the heat back on and add 1 cup boiled water, vinegar and salt. Let the mixture simmer for a 3-4 minutes, stirring occasionally.

9. When it starts to get thick, add a pinch of sugar and turn off the fire. Add the fried ginger, garlic and the ginger garlic paste.

10. Add the beef pieces. Stir well.

11. Let it cool and transfer to air tight glass jars.

Note

- I pressure cook the beef since the meat is tough, but ensure that it does not get over cooked and too soft, to a point where it breaks apart.

- You can use gingili oil for frying, but it has a rather strong flavor. So I use unflavoured oil for frying and the remaining steps in gingili oil.

- Instead of using chilli powder, you can opt to add whole dry red chilli. Soak the chilli in hot water for 30 minutes. Discard the water and grind it to a smooth paste. Sauté the chilli paste in oil.

Spiced Buttermilk (Sambharam)

 Sambharam is a refreshing drink to cool down your body on a hot summer day. It is also known as "*morum vellam*" in Kerala. The buttermilk is sprinkled with ginger, curry leaves and green chilli. I would recommend that you keep this in the fridge for some time before serving it.

Ingredients

- Yoghurt (1 cup)
- Water (2 cups)
- Curry leaves (2 sprigs)
- Ginger (½ inch piece)
- Green chilli (½)
- Shallots (2)
- Salt to taste

Method

1. Using a mortar and pestle, crush ginger, shallots, green chilli and curry leaves.
2. Blend the yoghurt in the mixer for few seconds.
3. Add 2 cups cold water and blend again.
4. Add the crushed mixture. Season with salt and transfer to a pitcher.
5. Refrigerate and serve chilled. You can strain the mix if you like.

Veppilakatti (Curry Leaf Chutney)

 The smell that wafts through the house when you fry curry leaves in coconut oil is sublime. This was one of the home made goodies that kept me going through my hostel days, back when I was in college. Our hostel food was not very inviting, but now looking back; it was here that I had some of my best meals and the best of times. The credit goes to my friends, the goodies from their homes and this vepillakatti. It goes best with plain rice, *manja moru* and beef cutlet. This combination surely takes me back to another time and place!

Ingredients

- Coconut oil (3 tbsp)
- Whole black pepper (2 tbsp)
- Curry leaves (3 handfuls)
- Grated coconut (1, large)
- Dry red chilli (a handful cut into pieces)
- Tamarind (size of a large gooseberry)
- Salt as required

Method

1. Heat oil in a large kadai. Add pepper and let it splutter.

2. Then add the grated coconut, dry red chilli, tamarind and salt.

3. Fry for a few minutes and add the curry leaves.

4. Keep stirring on low to medium heat till the coconut changes to dark brown color and the curry leaves turn crispy. This will take about 15 to 20 minutes.

5. Now remove from heat, let it cool and then grind this mixture to a coarse powder in the mixer. It needs to have a crunchy granular texture.

6. Store in an air tight container.

Brazilian Lemonade

 This is lemonade with a slight twist, but will be the creamiest and sweetest lemonade that you will ever try. It is like summer in a cup! One thing to keep in mind with regards to this drink is that letting this lemonade sit for more than a couple of hours can turn it bitter.

Ingredients

- Water (5 to 6 cups)
- Ice cubes (a large handful)
- Lime (5)
- Sugar (1 cup)
- Condensed milk (6 tbsp)

Method

1. Start by zesting all the lime skins. Zesting is the process of scraping off the yellow outer skin of the peel for use as flavoring.

2. Juice the limes.

3. In a mixer, add water, lime zest, lime juice, sugar and condensed milk.

4. Blend in the mixer for 10 seconds. This drink is best served immediately over ice.

Sharjah Shake

 Bangalore has many small local bakeries run by Malayalees. They have an amazing array of bakes, both sweet and savoury at very nominal rates. It was at one such bakery that I first tried the Sharjah shake. This banana and date smoothie is a tasty and creamy filling drink. Tale has it that this drink became popular during a Sharjah Cup cricket series and hence the name.

Ingredients

- Frozen milk (500 ml or 2 cups)
- Banana (1 cup)
- Dates (2-4, deseeded and skinned)
- Horlicks or Bournvita (2 tbsp)
- Sugar (1 tbsp or to taste)
- Cashew nuts (5-6)
- Peanut butter (1 tbsp, optional)

Method

1. Pour milk into Ziploc bags and keep in the freezer till it is semi frozen.

2. Into a blender, add the semi frozen milk, bananas, Bournvita, sugar, peanut butter and vanilla extract.

3. Blend into a smooth milkshake. Pour into a tall glass and enjoy.

4. You can add a scoop of ice-cream, some cashew nuts and a sprinkle of Bournvita on top. Serve chilled.

Note

- If the milk gets fully frozen, lightly crush it with a rolling pin and then add to the blender.

Garam Masala

 Garam masala is the quintessential everyday Indian spice mix. The flavor and fragrance of homemade masala powder is no comparison to masalas bought at the store. This spice blend is very popular in Indian households and used extensively in many curries. The mix of all the amazing spices makes the taste of this masala divine.

Ingredient

- Fennel seeds (½ cup or 60 grams)
- Cloves (10 grams)
- Star anise (5 pieces)
- Cardamom (20 grams)
- Nutmeg (½ piece)
- Cinnamon (4 sticks or 6 grams)
- Mace (2 pieces)

Method

1. In a heavy bottomed pan, dry roast the fennel seeds. Wait for the roasted smell to come through. This should take approximately 3 to 4 minutes. Transfer the fennel seeds to a bowl and allow to it cool.

2. Roast all the remaining ingredients together, until fragrant. This will again take about 2 to 3 minutes.

3. Transfer the whole spices along with the roasted fennel seeds and allow everything to cool.

4. In a mixer, grind the spices to a fine powder.

5. Store in an airtight container. This makes approximately 1 cup of masala powder.

Banana Jam

 You would think banana is a very unlikely fruit to make jam with, but that's not true at all. This banana jam has a deep mauve color and does not have a strong banana flavor. The *palayankodan* variety gives it a natural tanginess that makes it perfect for jams. These bananas are very rich in nutrients and largely found in southern India.

Ingredients

- Banana (5 kilos, small yellow variety called as *palayankodan*)
- Water
- Sugar (¼ quantity of the liquid measured)
- Cloves (4 to 5)

Method

1. Peel and cut the banana into small round pieces. Place it in a large pressure cooker and fill water up to the same level and pressure cook for two whistles.

2. When it cools down, strain the liquid through a sieve and measure the liquid.

3. Measure ¼ the quantity of that in sugar. (e.g., for 4 cups of liquid, add 1 cup of sugar).

4. Now boil this liquid on a high flame till it reaches half the quantity. Now add the measured sugar and continue to let it boil, while stirring.

5. Add 4-5 cloves. It will start to thicken into a jam like consistency. Turn off the heat and let it cool.

6. Fill into jars and store in a refrigerator. Since it does not contain any preservative, you will need to refrigerate it.

7. It will thicken further in the refrigerator. So don't let it get too thick on the stove.

Green Chutney

 Green chutney is a great spread for a quick sandwich. It can also be used as a dip for *samosas*. I love these quick and easy recipes which can be whipped up in few minutes.

Ingredients

- Coriander leaves (2 bunches)
- Mint leaves (10)
- Coconut (½ cup, grated)
- Tamarind (small piece)
- Shallots (2)
- Green chilli (1-2)
- Turmeric powder (¼ tsp)
- Ginger-garlic paste (½ tsp)
- Salt (½ tsp)
- Sugar (½ tsp)

Method

1. In a mixer, grind all the ingredients together. Adjust the salt and spice to your liking.

2. Spread on a sandwich with butter and enjoy.

Salted Caramel Sauce

 I have used this salted caramel sauce to layer the Banoffee Pie and Caramel Tart. It can also be used as a topping for ice creams and puddings. It is crucial to get the sugar caramelized to a rich amber colour to get the right flavor and consistency. You can store this sauce in the fridge for up to 2 weeks.

Ingredients

- Caster sugar (150 grams, sugar)
- Cream (90 ml, double cream or Amul fresh cream without the whey)
- Unsalted butter (60 grams)
- Salt to taste

Method

1. To make the caramel sauce; place the sugar in an even layer in a saucepan. On low heat, start cooking the sugar. If required, briefly swirl the sugar to help it along.

2. Once the sugar starts caramelizing, bring it to a deep amber color and remove from the heat.

3. In the meanwhile, heat the cream in the microwave until hot.

4. While whisking, gently pour the cream in a steady stream and stir well to combine. The sugar will bubble up, don't be alarmed!

5. Once it has completely combined, add butter and salt. Stir well. Once it has completely cooled, you can store in the fridge. It will thicken as it cools.

Note

- Caramel solidifies in the refrigerator so it needs to be reheated, either on the stove or in the microwave, until desired consistency is reached. Reheating the caramel will make it thinner and runnier.

Marinara Sauce

Meal prepping helps you cut down your kitchen time drastically. By preparing a large quantity of this versatile sauce, you can use it in your pastas, pizzas and pies whenever you need a quick meal. This sauce can be stored in the fridge for up to 3-4 days or up to a month in the freezer.

Ingredients

- Olive oil (2-3 tbsp)
- Fennel seeds (½ tsp)
- Onions (2, diced)
- Garlic paste (2 tsp)
- Tomato (5-6, skinned and pureed)
- Tomato ketchup (½ cup)
- Grated carrot (1 cup, optional)
- Red chilli flakes (1 tsp)
- Worcestershire sauce (1-2 tbsp)
- Nutmeg (½ tsp)
- Sugar (1 tsp – to balance the acidity)
- Black pepper powder (1 tsp)
- Salt to taste
- Hot water (1 cup)

Method

1. Heat olive oil in a pan and add fennel seeds. Now add onion and garlic paste and cook till the onions turn translucent.

2. Add grated carrot, tomato puree and tomato ketchup. Let it cook for few minutes. Then add 1 teaspoon of sugar and 1-2 tablespoon of Worcestershire sauce.

3. Add 1 cup hot water and bring to a gentle boil. Add oregano, nutmeg powder, Italian seasoning, salt and pepper.

4. Reduce the heat to low and simmer for 10 minutes till the mix thickens, stirring occasionally.

Note

- Grated carrot is completely optional and added to bulk up the sauce. You can also add other vegetables such as beetroot and capsicum.

White Sauce

 Also know as Béchamel sauce, this sauce forms the base in many pies and pastas. I have used this sauce in my Fish pie, Moussaka, Macaroni Shepherd's Pie, Creamy Spinach Pasta and Lasagna. For a richer version, use cream instead of milk. This recipe makes 1 cup of white sauce.

Ingredients

- Butter (2 tbsp)
- Garlic (½ tsp, minced)
- Plain flour (1 tbsp)
- Whole milk/cream (1 cup)
- Oregano/thyme/mixed herbs (½ tsp)
- Nutmeg (¼ tsp)
- Grated cheese (½ cup)
- Pepper (½ tsp)
- Salt

Method

1. Melt butter in a saucepan, add garlic and sauté.

2. On low heat, add the plain flour and stir for a minute until the raw smell of the flour dissipates.

3. To this, add cream/milk and mix well on low heat till it becomes a thick sauce. While still warm, add grated cheese. Stir well so that there are no lumps.

4. Sprinkle thyme, oregano, nutmeg, salt and pepper. It will thicken slightly as it cools down. Adjust the consistency by adding more milk if required. It will thicken as it rests.

Guacamole

 Guacamole is an avocado based dip or spread that you can have with chips or over toast. It is fresh, healthy and a must try whenever avocados are in season. Unlike most dips that tend to be unhealthy, avocados are highly nutritious. It's buttery texture and sweet nutty flavor makes it perfect for dips and spreads.

Ingredients

- Onion (1 small, diced)
- Red chilli (2, deseeded)
- Avocados (3, ripe)
- Coriander leaves (a handful)
- Cherry tomatoes (6 ripe)
- Juice of 1 lime
- Extra virgin olive oil (1 tbsp)
- Salt
- Pepper

Method

1. Soak the diced onion in cold water for 20 minutes to reduce the strong pungent flavor. Drain from water.

2. Scoop the flesh of the avocado and chop/mash it to a consistency that you like.

3. Combine the chopped coriander leaves, diced tomatoes, onion and mashed avocado.

4. Add the juice from 1 lime and 1 tablespoon of olive oil, then season with salt, black pepper and more lime juice, if needed.

5. Serve immediately.

Chocolate Cream Cheese Frosting

 There is no doubt that this is an indulgent frosting, but it is so worth it! It is slightly tangy and oozing with chocolate flavor. If you are a true chocolate fan, you will love it. Compliment this frosting with chocolate cake or vanilla cup cake, and it is pure heaven!

Ingredients

- Semi-sweet chocolate (170 grams, chopped)
- Unsalted butter (140 grams)
- Cream cheese (113 grams or ½ cup)
- Icing sugar (125 grams or 1 cup)
- Unsweetened cocoa powder (15 grams or 1/8 or cup)
- Hot brewed coffee (2 tbsp)

Method

1. Melt chocolate in the microwave, stirring every 30 seconds.
2. Cream butter and cream cheese until light, fluffy and pale yellow.
3. In a separate bowl, add 2 tablespoons of hot coffee to cocoa and stir.
4. Add the cooled chocolate and coffee mixture to the cream cheese mix.
5. Cream on to the lowest setting and add sugar, half cup at a time, until well incorporated. Frosting will darken as it sets.
6. Make sure the cakes are cool before frosting.

Measurement Equivalents

1/4 cup	62 ml
1/3 cup	83 ml
1/2 cup	125 ml
2/3 cup	167 ml
3/4 cup	188 ml
1 cup	250 ml
3 Teaspoons	1 Tablespoon
2 Tablespoons	1/8 cup
4 Tablespoons	1/4 cup
8 Tablespoons	1/2 cup
16 Tablespoons	1 cup
1 Teaspoon	5 ml
1 Tablespoon	15 ml
Tbsp	Tablespoon
Tsp	Teaspoon
ml	Milliliter
F	Fahrenheit
C	Celsius

Conclusion

 It has been a wonderful and exhilarating experience for me to put all these treasured recipes together. I do hope that this book will help you in your everyday cooking escapades! I also hope that you enjoy cooking and eating these dishes with your loved ones. For any clarifications on any of these recipes, you can reach out to me at *maryanngeo@gmail.com*.

All proceeds from the sale of this book will go towards the Kidney Warriors Foundation (KWF). KWF is the largest independent India-based network of kidney patients, caregivers, healthcare professionals and social workers who have voluntarily signed up to make a difference in the lives of people affected by kidney disease. Their main mission is to advocate for policies that improve access to health care and strengthen the quality of care for patients with kidney disease.

KWF also lends an arm of support to patients in desperate financial need. They seek financial assistance from families, friends and well-wishers to meet patients' urgent fund requests. For more details please visit *www.kidneywarriorsfoundation.org*

If you wish to make a donation to KWF, you can use the following details to do so.

Name:	Kidney Warriors Foundation
Bank:	HDFC
Branch:	Shoppers Stop Branch, Andheri (West), Mumbai
Account:	50200050993064
Account Type:	Current
IFSC:	HDFC0000114
MICR:	400240025

Thank you for your generosity.

Notes

Printed in Great Britain
by Amazon

71228204R00154